Proclaim Jubilee!

Other books by Maria Harris
published by Westminster John Knox Press

Fashion Me a People: Curriculum in the Church

Proclaim Jubilee!

A Spirituality
for the Twenty-first Century

Maria Harris

Westminster John Knox Press
Louisville, Kentucky

Scripture quotations from the New Revised Standard Version of the Bible are copyright © 1989 by the Division of Christian Education of the National Council of the Churches of Christ in the U.S.A. and are used by permission.

Grateful acknowledgment is made to Robert Bly for permission to reprint material from Antonio Machado, "Moral Proverbs and Folk Songs," in *Times Alone,* translated by Robert Bly (Middletown, Conn.: Wesleyan University Press, 1983).

Book design by Jennifer K. Cox
Cover design by Kevin Darst

First edition

Published by Westminster John Knox Press
Louisville, Kentucky

This book is printed on acid-free paper that meets the American National Standards Institute Z39.48 standard. ♾

PRINTED IN THE UNITED STATES OF AMERICA

96 97 98 99 00 01 02 03 04 05 — 10 9 8 7 6 5 4 3 2 1

Library of Congress Cataloging-in-Publication Data

Harris, Maria.
    Proclaim jubilee! : a spirituality for the twenty-first century / Maria Harris. — 1st ed.
        p.   cm.
    Includes bibliograpical references (p.) and index.
    ISBN 0-664-25661-9 (alk. paper)
    1. Spiritual life—Christianity. 2. Jubilee (Judaism)   I. Title.
BV4501.2.H3597   1996
263—dc20   96-277

In memory of Walter and Mary Tuohy

Contents

Foreword

My first hearing of this material was several years ago when Maria Harris presented the theme of Jubilee at my school, Columbia Theological Seminary. At that time, I found the lectures deeply moving in a way that was both energizing and invitational. Since that time, Harris has honed them further and advanced her thinking. But the main force of the materials, which I initially experienced, is present in their written form as well. Harris has written a classic at the convergence of scholarship, spirituality, and a passion for justice. The power of her writing lies in her refusal to stay safely and obediently within the confines of any of the usual divisions of labor.

To my mind, Harris's way of studying scripture is exactly as it ought to be. She has paid attention to the specificity of the text and is informed by sound critical study. But she will not stop there or let the text remain remote and distanced, as much critical study does. Without any heavy theory of inspiration, Harris responds to scripture as though it is a live, revelatory voice that illumines our present and generates futures for us that we could not have apart from the generativity of the text.

The theme of Jubilee is, of course, a many-faceted focus, exactly the kind of focus best suited to Harris's imaginative capacities. She understands how a particular ancient practice embodied in a particular text can take on a rich, dense life as an image, a symbol, and a metaphor. Moreover, Harris gives full play to the signing significance of the metaphor. But she never permits the metaphor to be cut off from its concrete sociopolitical placement so that it floats off into a contextless fantasy. In addition, Harris barely pauses to entertain the escapist question so often asked of the Jubilee tradition—"There is no evidence that they ever did it, is there?"—since she knows that whether it was ever "done" or not, it is there in the oldest dreams of Israel, waiting to be dreamed again, not perchance to sleep but in order to act.

The Jubilee themes that Harris takes up for explication are indeed deeply rooted in the text and, we may believe, in the practice of ancient Israel. This book shows the way in which these concrete practices are still urgent issues and choosable possibilities in our present time, which seems remote from that ancient, patriarchal, segmented, agrarian society. Harris's explication of the themes invites us, along with her, to "thick listening," which is one of her ways of speaking about prayer. This book is all about thick listening that understands and relishes the deep touch points that take place between suffering and imagination, touch points that can produce energy for "the healing of the world" that is now our urgent human vocation.

Land in fallowness is taken up by Harris as a rich and evocative program. It reminds us that the world (land) has a life of its own from the Creator, that it may not be farmed to death or used up to human advantage and indulgence. Beyond that, the fallowness necessary to land, which leads directly to the Sabbath principle, invites pondering of a whole way of existence that is infused with listening, waiting, and receiving. Thus Harris moves from the real estate of Palestine to "the land of ourselves, that tiny country each of us comprises." Land moreover requires a break in the fever of productivity and the tyranny of initiative taking in order to discover that there is something generative at work in creation that is not dependent on us but that hovers behind and before us, as behind and before all of God's earth. One can see in this representative discussion of Harris that the theme is richly loaded with perspective when handled by a poet such as Maria.

It is a leap from land to *forgiveness,* but Harris is attentive to the fact that the primary Jubilee text makes precisely that leap. For all of our usurpation of forgiveness into a theology of grace or into a calculating religion, it is clear that forgiveness has to do with land—owned, rented, borrowed, and mortgaged. So Harris, after the manner of the poets of graciousness, grows lyrical about forgiveness:

> forgive everything we can,
> forgive debts,
> forgive trespasses,
> forgive sins,

forgive family,
forgive world debt!

This is not, however, romantic: forgive the impossible, for it is the unforgivable that will finally crush whatever it is that is human about us. I find Harris's insight on forgiveness deeply moving and practically helpful. We do indeed live in a world of unrequited rage, unsatisfied hate, and unplumbed fear. Here, however, there is quite realistic and credible talk of breaking these vicious cycles and beginning again. Harris leads us to imagine a regiven innocence that jadedness seemingly can nullify, but because for-giving is re-giving, Harris suggests access to the gift that keeps on giving and re-giving and for-giving.

When we arrive at the theme of *liberation,* we expect to be on more familiar ground; except that we are again surprised, for Harris moves liberation to home and homecoming and to "coming home to one's self." At the brink of the familiar, this book again reverses field and thinks of those "far from home"—especially prisoners and children, who are the emblems of abuse and exploitation. And unless we ponder with some intentionality the "unhomedness" that our society regularly enacts in its dominant modes, we will miss the urgency of home for all of the displaced, whose numbers grow daily in unconscionable ways. As I read this, I became aware of how accustomed we have become, without noticing, to the notion that ours should be a society of general and programmatic displacement, wherein the absolute necessity of home becomes a luxury for only the advantaged and privileged. This book has a way of making the most ordinary assumptions we hold seem astonishing. And what we might at first think astonishing becomes ordinary when read through a Jubilee lens.

When Harris comes to *justice,* her fourth point of accent, she hits her stride. Justice is, of course, the core theme of Jubilee—except there is no "of course" for Harris. The notion of justice begins here in spirituality, and spirituality comes to be "our way of being in the world in light of the Mystery at the core of the universe; a mystery that some of us call God." This is about justice? Yes, about justice, because justice is not an extra or special ad hoc agenda but rather a steady way of being in the world. So Harris ponders "limits of accumulation," "creation of just possibilities," and being "willing to give." Harris presents the choice of Jubilee justice not as a terrible burden but as a realistic enactment of another way of living.

Perhaps the reader will sense my excitement about this book, because of the following points:

> Harris has refused to leave things in the conventional categories and so can bring matters into new relationships that quietly resketch our usual segmentations of the world.
>
> Harris is an addictive quoter, and given that effort on her part, *we* get the best from the most buoyant and inventive thinkers among us—Yoder and Moran and Thomas Berry and Arendt and Buber and Wendell Berry and Gutiérrez and Terrien and Walker and Dillard and Heschel—not to drop names but to place judicious reference, giving us pause and making us tremble.
>
> Harris is likewise a stunning phrase-spotter and phrase-maker, calling up and creating phrasing that brings everything abruptly into fresh focus. Try these: "tears of things" (Virgil), "heightened holy time," "I am becoming Jubilee," "to be forgiveness," "touch one Jubilee dimension and all the others quiver," "work of storying," "earth deficits," "a will can be a Jubilee document," "noisy spirituality." Reading Harris is like watching a poet arrange her scrapbook, one who carefully places each word and then annotates each phrase so that each gathers a world around itself.
>
> Harris has provided a full set of reflective questions at the end of each chapter. She knows there is more work to do in Jubilee, and she will not do it for us.

In the end, Jubilee is the liberty of gratitude, and *jubilation* its final expression. There are, to be sure, other, larger gratitudes in my life than *Proclaim Jubilee!* But this book will evoke the gratitude of the reader as it has mine. I think that is true for a very odd reason: there is peculiar convergence between the subject matter and the way it is written here. Harris not only writes about these things; she effects them! With a large gracefulness, the book is that kind of performative speech that is a doing. Response is not just gratitude to Harris, though there is that. It is also gratitude to the God present in these pages, to whom Harris pays simple, dense homage.

WALTER BRUEGGEMANN
COLUMBIA THEOLOGICAL SEMINARY

Preface

In 1992, I received a letter of invitation from a gifted former colleague, Joseph F. Kelly. Joe was living in Cleveland and serving as the chair of the Department of Religious Studies at John Carroll University, which had commissioned him to issue the invitation. "Would you be willing to come to our campus for a semester," his letter read, "teach one course, and give a series of lectures on a topic of your choice?" Then it continued, "Those would be your only duties, and you would be able to accomplish them in surroundings that include the resources of a major Jesuit university, the companionship of like-minded colleagues, and the artistic treasures of our city."

A teacher-writer's dream come true. I accepted. The absence of other commitments enabled me to take up residence at John Carroll for the entire fall semester of 1994. Almost three decades earlier, Walter J. Tuohy, who was chief executive officer of the Chesapeake and Ohio Railway, and his wife, Mary, had established the Tuohy Chair of Interreligious Studies that made my appointment possible, and when I arrived, I joined a long line of scholarly predecessors in holding that chair and engaging in work designed to contribute to religious understanding in our era.

Proclaim Jubilee! is the fruit of my work that semester. I had begun probes of the biblical Jubilee—for that was the "topic of my choice"—some years earlier and had already made forays into its implications for ecclesial life during brief periods when I delivered lectures at the Candler School of Theology in Atlanta; Columbia Seminary in Decatur, Georgia; Pittsburgh Theological Seminary; Brite Divinity School in Fort Worth; and Virginia Theological Seminary in Alexandria. I had also worked on Jubilee at Auburn Theological Seminary in New York and would do so again when I returned home, notably when Bob Reber, Barbara Wheeler, Larry

Rasmussen, Jim Forbes, Walter Wink, Dwayne Huebner, and Mark Wilhelm graciously spent an afternoon critiquing my next-to-final draft.

But in Cleveland I was given the opportunity to make Jubilee my main concern and to explore its meaning for persons and communities, including myself, who are facing the dawn of a new millennium. Appointment to the Tuohy Chair included the presentation of six public lectures that served as initial drafts of what eventually became this book. Not only did that public forum include insights from many of those who came to the lectures, it also helped me sharpen what were still inchoate hunches. In addition, participants were willing to sing along on occasion as together we incorporated the musical traditions of Jubilee into our meetings.

Additional help came from the library staff at John Carroll, especially Dr. Gorman Duffett and Nevin Mayer of the Grasselli Library, and from Christopher Merriman, my graduate assistant; Mary Sharon Shumacher in the Department of Religious Studies; Dr. Paul Lauritzen, who acted unfailingly as my guide in everything from finding directions to downtown Cleveland and scouting out the local Borders bookstore to fulfilling requests for the strange materials I sometimes needed for my class sessions; and from the hospitality of the distinguished teachers who made up my department, especially Paul, Tom Shubeck S.J., Doris K. Donnelly, and Joe Kelly, who taught me that the Jubilee tradition of care for the stranger was being exercised daily in my own personal life.

That and the other traditions of Jubilee—fallow land, forgiveness, freedom, justice, and jubilation—are the core of this book. In it I show how these traditions, when taken together, form a pattern for spirituality needed in the twenty-first century, while serving as avenues for educating in the direction of such a spirituality. I also suggest how to prepare for the 2000 Jubilee now, in personal, familial, communal, social, and economic life. And to help the reader in discerning the specifics of putting these suggestions into practice, I offer a series of questions for further reflection and conversation at the end of each chapter.

This means that in the hands of an individual reader or of a pastoral leader or religious educator, the book is a companion and a guide. Studied in a classroom, it is a source of reflection on both ancient and contemporary biblical sources. Read communally in parishes, congregations, religious orders, and ministering communities, it is a blueprint for attentive and aware response to the Jubilee vocation.

That vocation calls us to hold a yearlong Sabbath, forgive debts, and proclaim liberty throughout the land to all its inhabitants. It impels us to do justice. And finally, it persuades us to hold a great feast and throw a grand party, adding our voices to the growing chorus of Jubilee people who sing the festive and grateful prayer of praise and delight, "Jubilate Deo, omnis tera." Praise God, all the earth, and all peoples of the earth. For a Jubilee appears in our age. It shall be holy to you.

MARIA HARRIS
MONTAUK, NEW YORK
FEBRUARY 1996

1

Themes in a Century: Challenges for Jubilee

In this book I explore the biblical Jubilee as both a pattern of spirituality and a model for religious education and ministry. Almost two decades ago I began this exploration with an initial search into how the practice of Sabbath influences and nourishes Western religious life. Inevitably, that search led me to the "Sabbath of Sabbaths," the Jubilee year described in the twenty-fifth chapter of the book of Leviticus. There I discovered that Jubilee and Sabbath were intertwined, and that the biblical Jubilee actually begins with the LORD saying to Moses on Mount Sinai, "When you enter the land that I am giving you, the land shall observe a sabbath for the LORD" (Lev. 25:1–2).

Then the instruction continues, "Six years you shall sow your field, and six years you shall prune your vineyard, and gather in their yield; but in the seventh year there shall be a sabbath of complete rest for the land, a sabbath for the LORD" (3–4). Eventually, the instruction culminates in the command:

> You shall count off seven weeks of years, seven times seven years, so that the period of seven weeks of years gives forty-nine years. Then you shall have the trumpet sounded loud; on the tenth day of the seventh month—on the day of atonement—you shall have the trumpet sounded throughout all your land. And you shall hallow the fiftieth year and you shall proclaim liberty throughout the land to all its inhabitants.
>
> (8–10a)

Intrigued by the instruction to hallow the fiftieth year, I have described—in an earlier book—what this command means for women
who have counted off seven years of seven years, celebrated our fiftieth birthdays, and entered the fullness of age.[1] In *Proclaim Jubilee!*
however, I take another perspective and a different point of departure. I ask readers to attend with me to Jubilee's implications in the
wider, broader arena of our entire society. I ask readers to consider
with me what Jubilee means—politically, economically, and
morally—for all of us, not only over-fifty individuals but families,
religious congregations, institutions, and nations. I ask how living
the Jubilee might affect our schooling, our economies, our families.
I ask how it might affect the prisoners in our jails and the children
on our streets.

Biblical references

Studying Leviticus 25 and related scripture texts, especially the
fourth chapter of Luke's Gospel and the sixty-first chapter of Isaiah, and reading contemporary commentators on Jubilee, I have become convinced that Jubilee provides avenues for educating religiously and interreligiously and that instead of being an obsolete
set of pathways belonging exclusively to an ancient people who
never really tried them (as some argue), it is—or can be—a richly
textured, vital response to the challenges of our era and the complex issues of contemporary life.

I am also convinced that Jubilee teaching qualifies as a comprehensive spirituality with profound implications for religious existence in today's world. I believe that as a spirituality attentive to
dailiness, flesh, and blood, it constitutes "a way of being in the
world in the light of the Mystery at the core of Creation"—the
shorthand meaning I give to the term spirituality.[2]

In the chapters that follow, I describe what this can mean for
those discovering the vocation of proclaiming Jubilee. Drawing on
biblical, ecclesial, and theological sources, I make specific suggestions concerning the kinds of education that foster and encourage
the practice of Jubilee. These suggestions arise, in turn, from probing Jubilee's core teachings, which are as follows:

> You shall let the land lie fallow, that is, you shall
>   practice Sabbath;
> You shall forgive debts, letting forgiveness in;
> You shall free captives and proclaim liberty;

> You shall find out what belongs to whom and give
>   it back (a phrase inspired by the work of Walter
>   Brueggemann);[3]
> You shall hold a great feast, learning to sing the can-
>   ticle of "Jubilate."

The Force of the Times

Before moving directly to these Jubilee teachings, however, I want to situate our relation to them by attending to the times. Not only do we bring our personal, social, and geographic locations to Jubilee, we bring our *temporal* locations too. That means we carry with us the realities of the late twentieth century as it shades into the twenty-first. We are communities made up of women and men standing on a pristine border whose boundary is the end of one century and the beginning of a new one; the end of one millennium and the beginning of another. We cannot respond to the call of Jubilee without addressing the prophetic, moral, and spiritual force that such an end time/beginning time carries.

The work of the poet Carolyn Forché is filled with a similar conviction: we are marked and affected by the times in which we live, not only by the places.[4] Our times shape us; to use language from Martin Buber, they "inflict destiny" on us and are "words demanding an answer happening to us."[5] Moreover, just as they have for earlier people in other ages, our times demand a response in their own way, reminding us that not only do the people of our era have a unique identity, the era has a unique identity too.

Half a century ago playwright Christopher Fry captured the force one's times can have. At the end of Fry's play *A Sleep of Prisoners,* the character of Joe Meadows, oldest of the four prisoners of war whose lives have alternated between sleep and waking during the drama, speaks these lines:

> The human heart can go to the lengths of God.
> Dark and cold we may be, but this
> Is no winter now. The frozen misery
> Of centuries breaks, cracks, begins to move,
> The thunder is the thunder of the floes,
> The thaw, the flood, the upstart Spring.

Thank God our time is now when wrong
Comes up to face us everywhere,
Never to leave us till we take
The longest stride of soul men ever took.
Affairs are now soul size.
The enterprise
Is exploration into God.[6]

Ironically, Meadows's reflection applies to time throughout human history: the times have always come up to meet us and affairs have always been "soul size." The task has always been an exploration of the ways a living God summons human beings to fidelity. If I take my own Christian tradition as an illustration, its history makes this clear. As the first millennium C.E. began, Jesus of Nazareth was bringing a world of challenge into civilization, a new set of scriptures was being recorded, and a new religious community was trying to figure out its relation to Judaism. And once the second millennium dawned and then became the full light of day, the church moved into scholasticism, the stirrings that would become the Renaissance, and eventually a religious reformation.

It is far too soon to tell—perhaps even to imagine—what awaits us in the third millennium. Nevertheless, the century now ending and the new era about to begin have their own constellation of factors. To contextualize the subsequent chapters on Jubilee, I describe below one such constellation that exists today. Admittedly, the constellation is incomplete, and readers will want to include other themes, especially where our social and geographical locations differ. Nevertheless, each of the themes I name has a universal resonance that demands religious response as this century ends and the new one begins. Each acts as a challenge to religious and/or spiritual people everywhere, a challenge to which, in subsequent chapters, I propose the response of Jubilee.

These themes include a political-economic demand, an emphasis in living humanly, a sobering corrective, a creative power, and a religious vocation. The demand is *liberation;* the emphasis is *connectedness;* the corrective is *suffering;* the power is *imagination;* and the vocation is *tikkun olam*—the repair of the world. I turn to these now as themes in a century that act as profound challenges for the era that will dawn with the year 2000.

Liberation

Religious historians of our century have already made it clear that beginning in the 1960s and continuing through to today, the theology of liberation reshaped the religious landscape throughout the world. Beginning in Latin America, calls for freedom were articulated by the poorest of the poor, notably in the small Christian communities that emerged in countries such as Brazil. Gustavo Gutiérrez of Peru gave voice to the movement and brought it to international attention in his magisterial work *A Theology of Liberation*,[7] even as Catholic episcopal conferences meeting in Medellín, Colombia, and Puebla, Mexico, confirmed the movement and gave it official sanction. Eventually, and often through the influence of the basic Christian community movement—the *comunidades de base*—liberation as a religious reality encircled the globe.

By the beginning of the 1990s, reports Robert McAfee Brown, one of the U.S. theologians most conversant with liberation theology, theologians from Soweto to Managua to Manila to Seoul called for freedom and liberation "out of their struggles against racial, economic and political injustice."[8] Those calls have been expressed in many ways, including three significant documents. In 1985, South African theologians produced *The Kairos Document: A Challenge to the Churches*, demanding the end of apartheid; in 1988, *Kairos Central America: A Challenge to the Churches of the World* urged Central American churches to give primary religious, theological, and economic attention to the poor; and in 1989 with *Kairos International*, contributors from the Philippines, South Korea, Namibia, South Africa, El Salvador, Guatemala, and Nicaragua stressed the conviction that the liberation sought by the poor is not only religious but political and economic. That third Kairos document notes that in our era, colonialism "involves economic rather than political control. . . . It features multinational corporations, unfair trade barriers and military bases with nuclear weapons throughout the world."[9] The document voices the belief that in response to these situations, and in resistance to growing imperialism, the movement of liberation by a conscious, organized people "marks the coming of age of a new historical subject."[10]

In education, such a coming of age has been described and articulated by Brazilian educator Paulo Freire in what is one of the great twentieth-century educational classics, *Pedagogy of the Oppressed.*[11] In this book, and in other subsequent works, Freire describes the power of a literacy that enables reading one's entire world as well as printed texts. Philosopher Freire—his practice and philosophy of education so commanding he has often landed in prison—condemns what he calls the "banking theory" of education: placing material inside someone's head to be drawn out when an exam comes around, just as, in modern banking, a check is written in order to draw out money. In its stead he proposes "dialogical" education, a form of education that is based on the belief that every human person, by reason of his or her existence, has a "vocation to be a subject"—not an object. This approach offers liberation as a pedagogical outcome.

Here in the United States we have our own examples. The civil rights movement of the second part of this century, forever stained by the blood of many martyrs, has legally changed the lives of countless African Americans, even while many U.S. citizens know that much more needs to be done. The Reverend Jesse Jackson embodies this "much more" as he continues to challenge systemic and institutional racism, traveling to school after school in this nation and teaching young people to say, "I am Somebody"—that is, "I have a vocation to be a subject." Persons with disabilities find ramps and curbside crossings available for wheelchairs—ramps and crossings that are modern sacramentals. They also find job opportunities in unprecedented numbers, liberated through legislation that mandates such opportunity. Gay and lesbian men, women, and teenagers also find unprecedented protection under law, although their fight for liberation and their fear that protective legislation will be overturned continues too. And in one of the most significant movements of liberation of the twentieth century—for many, *the* most significant—women, old and young, of every race and class, have declared to government, the military, business, religion, and all other institutions that our second-class status is over. In this century, when we have finally become free to exercise the franchise as adult citizens, women here and throughout the world are at last making the full, human contributions that resistant societies have too long refused to accept. As the century ends, the voices of women and girls are among the loudest, clearest, and strongest insisting, "I am Somebody."

My point is that liberation is a theme of our time—perhaps *the*

theme. But it is also central to the spirituality of Jubilee. We return to it directly when we consider freedom in chapter 4, but liberation is not found only or exclusively in the proclamation of freedom. Instead, it exists in all the other Jubilee tenets. We shall discover that it appears in resting the land and thus liberating it, in forgiveness, in justice, and in jubilation.

Connectedness

There is a sense in which the early decades of our century centered on the individual. In Western society we focused on the emergence of the ego, and in the world community we championed the revelation of ourselves as subjects, not objects. As with liberation, the discoveries weren't new, although the widespread acceptance of individual psychological therapy was, proving to be an important source of personal wholeness. In our times, millions of people have been healed of debilitating trauma by addressing broken parts of themselves.

But in recent decades criticism of such healing work as being narcissistic or overindulgent is heard. Self-help groups are being closely scrutinized;[12] *I'm Dysfunctional, You're Dysfunctional* is the title of a recent book,[13] and an earlier one lamented *The Culture of Narcissism*.[14] The criticism found in these books arises at least in part from a growing awareness that the personal psyche's "shadow" side represents more than a hidden part of oneself. All of us also represent hidden parts of one another to one another. Poet Antonio Machado suggests:

> Look for your other half
> Who walks always next to you
> And tends to be who you aren't.[15]

The word *individual* gives way to *person* here, and *person*, by definition, means someone in connection, someone who realizes that *esse est co-esse*—to be is to be with. I am Somebody, yes, but I do not stand alone in isolated individualism. Instead, I am Somebody who is your sister or your brother. I remind you—as well as myself—that all reality is relational. Rodney King put this with extraordinary eloquence during the Los Angeles riots in April 1992, sounding like a character from a Samuel Beckett play: "We're all stuck here together," he pleaded. "Can't we try to get along?"

As the century comes to an end, connectedness dominates our thinking in another way as well, as we recognize it extending beyond us humans to the planet—presaging another Jubilee tradition, "Let the land lie fallow." Where human beings once exploited nature thoughtlessly or in the belief that no great harm could be done to the environment, the twentieth century is leaving us with a transforming of such unconsciousness. We now recognize we have an intimate connection with air, water, soil, fire, everything— a connection summed up in Celie's last letter in *The Color Purple*: "Dear God. Dear stars, dear trees, dear sky, dear peoples. Dear Everything. Dear God."[16]

The Rio Earth Summit of the early nineties, a gathering of persons from around the world concerned with environmental issues, and countless environmental experts who are speaking today assure us that the global ecosystem includes all of us, and if one goes, we all go. Dennis Meadows, one of three authors of the "limits to growth" thesis put forth over two decades ago, says we thought then we had time until around 2030 or 2040 in which to fashion a society that did not destroy the earth's resources such as water, land, and air. Now he thinks it looks like a new set of attitudes must be in place in a much shorter time—perhaps by 2012.[17]

One description of the face of connectedness as we encounter it today comes from Padraic O'Hare, professor at Merrimack College in Massachusetts. In January 1991, the day after Operation Desert Storm started, when O'Hare walked into his religious studies classroom he was tempted to discuss the onset of the Gulf War to see what the students were thinking and how they were reacting. But on second thought, he suggested to the class that they pray. Their praying would not be an attempt at magical manipulation of the Divine, he explained—a God who could have prevented Desert Storm would have done so. Instead, he suggested they pray because prayer can make us attentive, mindful.

Prayer can make us pause, can slow us down, can assist us in "thick" listening. Prayer is, or can be, a special kind of awareness, for if and when we pray—with the eyes and heart of a bodhisattva—we become cognizant that we are all implicated in any action taken by even a single one of us. Human, we belong to a species where one act of compassion has ramifications for everyone on the planet; where one act of cruelty touches us all. Such awareness, O'Hare told his students, might enable them to attend not just to waging peace or to making peace but to *being* peace.[18]

Drawing on the thought of the Buddhist monk Thich Nhat Hanh, O'Hare told the students Desert Storm was like the sheet of paper he was holding in his hand. Then he quoted Nhat Hanh's teaching:

> If you are a poet, you will see clearly that there is a cloud floating in this sheet of paper. Without a cloud, there will be no rain; without rain, the trees cannot grow; and without trees, we cannot make paper. The cloud is essential for the paper to exist.
>
> If we look into this sheet of paper even more deeply, we can see the sunshine in it. Without sunshine, the forest cannot grow. And so, we know that the sunshine is also in this sheet of paper. . . . And if we continue to look, we see the logger who cut the tree and brought it to the mill to be transformed into paper. And we will see wheat. The logger cannot exist without his daily bread, and therefore the wheat that became his bread is also in this sheet of paper. The logger's father and mother are in it too.[19]

Then O'Hare made the connection. On that cold and frightening January morning, he told his students, "We are all in Operation Desert Storm."[20]

In the chapters that follow, we will see how this theme of connectedness acts as a challenge to the human community today and how it reoccurs throughout Jubilee, especially in letting the land lie fallow, in forgiveness, and in the search for justice. Now, however, I turn to a third theme. Along with liberation and connectedness, the twentieth century challenges us with the sobering corrective of suffering.

Suffering

People who realize the imperative to become involved in lessening the evil in the world often want to move into action immediately, especially if raised in the "can-do" United States. Liberation and connectedness push in this direction. But the twentieth century has intensified awareness of a third reality throughout our world, an awareness made sharper and more pervasive than in earlier ages because of mass communication. This is the recognition of the omnipresence of pain and suffering, of what the poet Virgil called *lacrimae rerum*, "the tears of things." The century is leaving us with the sobering corrective of suffering, cautioning us to walk slowly and gently, to cultivate stillness, to draw on inner gifts, even as we move, as we must, to respond to suffering. (Let us not understand too quickly: we must love one another or die; in the face of suffering, we must act. But there is wisdom too in the familiar proverb turned back on itself: "Don't just do something. Stand there.") This corrective reminds us that before the miseries of the world no easy answers exist, and the gifts of all peoples are needed in any attempts to heal brokenness.

Although much of the closing century impels us toward liberation and connectedness, the century also ends bloodied and disfigured, demonstrating enormous resistance to those same movements. Two world wars testify, one ending in an armistice that did not hold, the other ending with unbelievable carnage in the firebombing of civilian populations such as those of Dresden and Hamburg and the destruction not only of the cities but of the people of Hiroshima and Nagasaki. Bosnia testifies, Kuwait testifies, Rwanda testifies. Vietnam testifies too, both to the ruin of that country and to the ruptures the war brought to the United States, their pain laid too heavily on the war's veterans and their spouses, parents, children. A core of unbelievable horror, the Holocaust of European Jews, remains a fissure of evil unfathomable, inexpressible, incomprehensible, scarring the face of the twentieth century.

I include suffering as one of the twentieth-century themes that acts as a challenge before the approaching Jubilee, because suffering adds another element to the closing century's constellation of forces: our awareness of the pain and death surrounding us. Before choosing actions that address the pain and death, suffering demands two prior responses.

First, it makes us stop; it slows us down. When human suffering confronts us and we are in its presence, we find ourselves bereft of ordinary ways of responding. Pain and a violent or unnecessary death, although constant, are not *ordinary,* not *usual.* They demand alternatives, options beyond small talk. They point toward silence, a reverent, prayerful silence; and they point toward ritual, especially rituals of mourning, grieving, and weeping.

Second, suffering is our entry into fear and dread. When it arrives, we can't see its outcome. We're rarely sure what it means, but we *are* certain we don't like it. In 1973, Ernest Becker wrote a Pulitzer Prize–winning book, *The Denial of Death*, studying this issue. He pointed out that facing our experiences of both life and death means facing the *terror* of existence, often so difficult we drink and drug ourselves out of that encounter, or spend our time consuming goods, which can amount to the same thing.[21]

With reference to the belief that suffering demands silence and ritual, it is important to note that when we become aware of suffering demanding response, we often *can't* act because we haven't mourned or grieved. One of the great contributions in this century of the action for justice designed by those with a liturgical grounding is that regularly, before a demonstration to protest or say, "Stop!" to the madness of selling arms, denying health care to children, or killing someone who's killed someone else—as in the application of the death penalty—the so-called activists pray, keep vigil, and mourn, often all night, because suffering demands such ritual. Anyone who has made the prayerful procession down to that great sacrament of healing, the Vietnam Memorial, and traced the names of the dead with their fingertips knows the power of such ritual.

With reference to facing the terror of existence, suffering teaches something else: not to face it alone, either personally or as communities, because response to suffering needs the wisdom of all peoples. When the World Council of Churches met in Sydney, Australia, more than a decade ago, Krister Stendahl, then dean of Harvard Divinity School, noted that whenever an issue was brought to the table, it got four characteristic responses: Latin Americans responded with customary passion; Africans asked what the implications were for the community; Asians reflected quietly in contemplative mindfulness; and North Americans inquired, "What are we going to *do?*"[22] The point of this recollection is not to set these responses in conflict. Instead, it is to note that we need all four perspectives. We need passion *and* community *and* contemplative being *and* active intervention when responding to suffering.

These issues reappear when we come to the Jubilee injunctions to let the land lie fallow and to face the tasks of prophetic justice that constitute finding out what belongs to whom and giving it back. They also permeate the repentance and lamentation that are factors in forgiveness. They even reappear in the final command to hold a great feast and sing "Jubilate," and in the discovery that our tears can be turned into dancing when we attend to building the city of God.

In preparation for those traditions, however, and as we gather the wisdom of many peoples to fashion responses to suffering, we find ourselves incorporating ways of acting characteristic of a fourth theme. In the light of liberation, connectedness, and the sobering corrective of suffering, our century provokes us to draw on the creative powers that have been unleashed during its nine-and-a-half decades. Our era instructs us in using the artistic imagination.

Imagination

In many ways, the twentieth century has created the conditions for a festival of the imagination. As the century ends, individual artists such as James Lee Byars, George Baselitz, and Nancy Rubin have forced new visions on us,[23] even as popular art in such countries as Chile, Zaire, and Nicaragua has produced work through which peasants and workers confront political oppression.[24] In addition, science and technology have generated unparalleled invention whose end is nowhere in sight, and photography, film, and television have made the mass communication of images a daily occurrence.

Like all important realities, the imagination generating such work is complex and ambiguous. Reflecting on its positive, re-creative power, Paul Ricoeur has written that the imagination is the center of the profound workings that impel decisive changes in our visions of the world. Arguing that every real conversion occurs first at the level of our directive images, Ricoeur believes that human beings can alter reality by altering their imaginations, and that "in imagining possibilities, human beings act as prophets of their own existence."[25]

The imagination can also have tremendous political power. Susan Sontag, reflecting on the problematic nature of photography, nevertheless honors the assumption that even a still photograph can capture a privileged moment and then make that moment accessible to millions. As an example, she suggests that "photographs like the one that made the front page of most newspapers in the world in 1972—a naked South Vietnamese child just sprayed by American napalm, running down a highway toward the camera, her arms open, screaming with pain—probably did more to increase the public revulsion against the war than a hundred hours of televised barbarities."[26]

Similarly, the image of the lone, silent figure standing with unyielding courage before the tanks in Tiananmen Square in China's 1989 student uprising attuned the world through a single image to the nature of that uprising. And the image of the earth as seen from the moon sends incontrovertible evidence to everyone who studies it that in space we dwell in a sea of connectedness, without any original boundaries between us.

In contrast, what are we to make of imagination and the role of images in other settings? Three events, close in time to one another, forced many to ask this in the summer of 1994. In late June, millions of people all over the world watched for hours as a white Ford Bronco sped along the Santa Monica Freeway. The orgy of watching concluded as viewers shifted compulsively to as many as eight channels while the natural light faded, in order to look at live footage of a parked car in the driveway of a Brentwood, California, house.[27]

Later, in one brief week at the end of July, we were given images far more awesome and horrifying. Astronomers said they "had never seen anything" like the explosions occurring when chunks of comet crashed into the planet Jupiter, one of the chunks as large as an alp, at exactly the same time relief workers were signaling to the world that they "had never seen anything" like the cataclysm of Rwanda, with its overflow of violent death and its hundreds of thousands of terrified refugees fleeing from butchery.[28]

These events illustrate the power of images. But they can also make us pause to consider a danger they create. Essayist Paul Gray pursues this, writing that "the danger of images lies not in the information they carry but rather in our propensity to believe—once we have seen them—that we have seen the whole picture." The truth, he concludes, is that with the much-heralded visual age upon us, we need to remember "that images do not come with built-in memories or instructions in how they should be read. If we are to understand them correctly, we must still do that work ourselves."[29]

The imagination is the seat of such work. But ironically, the very word *imagination* can sometimes short-circuit our creative power, because imagination emphasizes imaging, seeing, and envisioning. That may cause an imbalance, an overemphasis on *looking* wherein imagination, disconnected from the rest of the body, can distance us from life. This is a point I take W. B. Yeats as making in his prayer "God save us from the thoughts we think in the mind alone. Those who sing a lasting song sing in the marrow bone."[30] Yeats isn't against the mind—or the eyes. But he is against narrowing human imagination, insisting that it include all the power of the human body, and all the power of the body politic too.

Therefore I would add the word *artistic to imagination*, because artistry means bodily *involvement*. Not only does artistry assume the hearing, gesture, and bodily movement of music and dance; artistry also celebrates touch as in sculpture, place as in architecture, the "feeling with the eye" needed for painting, the power of voice and ear essential to poetry, drama, and literature. Artistry celebrates the connections among and the liberating possibilities of all those bodily powers leading to the "creation of form expressive of human feeling" that is the work of art.[31]

The pertinence of this meaning of art at the end of the century lies in art's emphasizing a set of powers other than vision and dreaming, science and technology. Without denying them, it insists on a deeper dimension. Artistic imagination may begin with dreams and visions, but it never ends with them. Instead, artistic imagination demands that visions and dreams be fleshed out in concrete, bodily forms that attend to touch and place and voice. So I name the artistic imagination as a challenge for Jubilee because Jubilee is, preeminently, a set of bodily actions—not only a seeing but a solid and particular doing that is incarnated in the bodily practices of blowing trumpets and proclaiming freedom, asking and granting forgiveness, doing the works of mercy that serve justice, and preparing for a great feast, filled with song, celebration, and praise.

The Repair of the World

Such physical actions are the stuff of the last theme I shall mention, the religious vocation directed to healing the world. Earlier in this century, Joseph Stalin reportedly asked sarcastically, "How many divisions has the Pope?" dismissing his religious power; similarly, at the CIA thoughtful suggestions to study Islamic religious leaders under the Shah were rejected as mere "sociology." Both are examples of the dismissal of religion on the world scene in favor of economics, military might, and politics.

But as the cold war has ended and religious conflicts have taken center stage in the world, new attention to the power of religion grows. The Center for Strategic and International Studies based in Washington, D.C., for example, has labeled religion "the missing dimension of statecraft" and faulted both the underestimation of religious differences as a source of conflict and the neglect of religious traditions, institutions, and leaders as catalysts in ending warfare or bringing about peaceful democratic change.[32] At the personal level, women and men are giving renewed attention to spiritual hungers within ourselves, signaling desire for depth in our personal lives on one hand and awareness of realms greater than ourselves on the other.

In other words, many people today are acknowledging—as persons, as communities, as nations—the existence of the reality of a "call," a religious vocation. When this vocation goes awry or is truncated, it can result in fear, stagnation, and violence. When it is healthy, however, it is a force calling for response to liberation, to connectedness, and to suffering both within and beyond ourselves, through the use of creative power. The healthy religious vocation I name as most consonant with Jubilee is deeply sedimented in Jewish and Christian tradition. This vocation, often presented as a creation story, is itself a result of artistic imagination and is described in Jewish lore as *tikkun olam*—the repair of the world.

The seventeenth-century Jewish mystic Isaac Luria spins a story describing *tikkun olam*. In the beginning, he says, the Creator of the universe, deciding to make a world, drew in the divine breath—contracted—in order to make room for the creation coming into being. In this enlarged space the Creator then set vessels and into the vessels poured the brilliance of the divine light. The light was too brilliant for the vessels, however, and unable to contain it, they shattered all over the universe. Since that time, the myth continues, the work of the human beings has been to go about the universe, picking up the shards of creation and trying to mend and transform the vessels by refashioning them in a work known as "the repair of the world."[33]

As we end the twentieth century and begin the twenty-first, suffering teaches us that we move about in a shattered world with

unnumbered shards at our feet and wrong coming up to meet us
everywhere. But we also move about as liberated subjects, knowing
that we are connected to one another and the earth; knowing too
that a living God has placed the power of artistic imagination in our
souls. This end time/beginning time is a heightened, deepened
kairos time, a time of destiny.

As we confront this destiny, we can be certain that even our
finest attempts at restoring the shattered vessels will never completely remove the lines of breakage. Old cracks will remain; new
seams and fault lines will develop. Still, that ought not preclude our
acting, for if we attempt repair, our fingerprints will be on the vessels and our lives and our work will matter, to ourselves, to the next
generations, and to our fragile planet.

A Proposal

As a vehicle for this work of repair, I propose the biblical Jubilee.
In the decades to come, any education that is religious and any spirituality that is whole will need to attend to each of the themes I have
named in this introductory chapter. They will also need to detect,
and sniff out those signs of flakiness, romanticism, or sentimental-
ity that make education false and spirituality cheap.

In addition, true religious education and genuine spirituality
will have to foster the kind of artistic, creative power that is not
only in the mind but sedimented in bodily practice as a lasting
song in the marrow bone of contemporary life. There will have to
be education and spirituality that are both mystical and political,
although political-religious life is often unaware of its own privilege, and mystical-religious life is often unaware of a social
world.[34]

This is precisely where Jubilee comes in—healing and joyous,
but not sentimental; hard and difficult, yet ultimately a specific,
concrete set of responses to the cries of the earth and of all who inhabit it. Eventually, Jubilee ushers in an era of forgiveness, freedom, justice, and jubilation. It begins, however, with a not-doing:
the decision to pause and to let the land lie fallow. It begins in stillness. It begins—as we shall see in the next chapter—with a Sabbath
that readies us for the next decade, the next century, and the next
millennium.

For Further Reflection and Conversation

1. As you read this chapter, which of the contemporary themes noted here—liberation, connectedness, suffering, imagination, repair of the world—seemed most important to you, most crucial? Can you say why?

2. Which of the themes is most central in your own life and in the life of your family and community?

3. What themes do you believe it is important to add to the constellation of liberation, connectedness, suffering, imagination, and repair of the world as the year 2000 approaches? Why do you include these additional themes?

4. What meaning do you give to the word *education?*

5. How is education a part of your personal life? How is it a part of your community life?

6. What meaning do you give to the word *spirituality?*

7. How is spirituality manifested in your personal life? How is it manifested in your community life, including the community of your nation?

2

Let the Land Lie Fallow

Prelude

Some years ago, I worked with a pastor who believed that religious traditions hold flash points within them. He told me that when the times are ripe and people in these traditions arrive at a particular moment in history, the flash points go off. They erupt like starbursts or like glorious fireworks, because the world is ready for them. This happens not only in a few concentrated areas but in widely scattered locations around the globe.

Jubilee is emerging as such a series of flash points today. This book does not represent an isolated attempt to kindle interest in this biblical teaching, nor am I a lone adherent preoccupied with promoting it. Instead, over the last two decades, and even more loudly as the millennium approaches, the Jubilee trumpet has been sounding everywhere.

Internationally respected religious leaders such as Emilio Castro and Mortimer Arias and scholars such as André Trocmé, John Howard Yoder, Sharon H. Ringe, and Dorothee Soelle have examined Jubilee in their writings.[1] The World Council of Churches gave it serious consideration as the theme of its 1998 South Africa meeting. And Pax Christi USA dedicated the year from August 1994 to August 1995 (the latter being the fiftieth anniversary of the Hiroshima and Nagasaki bombings) as a Jubilee year, pledging "to use the time to grow in commitment to nonviolence through prayer, education, organizing and witnessing to the God of life and resisting the forces of violence that threaten our communities, nation and world."[2]

In addition, the Evangelical Lutheran Church in America (ELCA) has used Jubilee in a countrywide gathering as the basis for its educational efforts of teaching to reach, linking five different Lutheran centers through teleconferencing to do so.[3] Herman Daly, formerly of the World Bank, and Alvin Schorr of Columbia University, both secular economists, have posed Jubilee as a model for programs that reduce income inequality.[4] Panamanian missionaries have called for a Jubilee year during which the crushing national debt of many Latin American countries would be forgiven.[5] And the Vatican has begun preparing for what the pope is calling "the grand Jubilee of the year 2000." Its proposed design includes prayer, repentance for the church's sins over the past two thousand years, and reconciliation with other religious bodies by the worldwide Roman Catholic Church as the millennium arrives.[6]

At the same time, ordinary religious folk such as Jewish thinker Arthur Waskow and farmer-theologian Richard Cartwright Austin are proposing Jubilee spirituality as a resource for our times,[7] even as parishes, local church staffs, and denominational boards consider the act of declaring a Jubilee year—or at the very least a Jubilee time—to focus on the religious ways of being in the world that constitute Jubilee teaching.[8]

As these flash points erupt around the globe, in worldwide organizations and in daily personal life, three biblical texts provide primary guidance. In this chapter I cite these texts, each of which openly proclaims the Jubilee. Then I move to Jubilee's starting point—letting the land lie fallow—and probe the twofold meaning of this phrase. Finally, I examine Sabbath, the essential preliminary condition not only for fallow land but for each of the subsequent Jubilee traditions: forgiveness, freedom, justice, and jubilation.

Texts for the Jubilee

Of the three scripture texts from which Jubilee radiates, one is from the New Testament and two are from the Hebrew Bible. Luke 4:16–20 describes Jesus returning to Nazareth where he was brought up and going to the synagogue on the Sabbath as was his custom. When the time comes, he unrolls the scroll of the prophet Isaiah and finds the place where it is written:

> The Spirit of the LORD is upon me,
> because he has anointed me
> to bring good news to the poor.

> He has sent me to proclaim release to the captives
> and recovery of sight to the blind,
> to let the oppressed go free,
> to proclaim the year of the LORD's favor.

Then he rolls up the scroll, gives it back to the attendant, and sits down. With the eyes of everyone in the synagogue fixed on him, he makes the stunning proclamation, "Today this scripture has been fulfilled in your hearing."

The second text is the reading from Third Isaiah chosen by Jesus on that Sabbath. Although he also included a citation from 58:6, the central text he chose was from chapter 61, which bears a critical phrase that Jesus repeated: "to proclaim the year of the LORD's favor." As Jesus surely knew, Isaiah's teaching flowered into a powerful and poetic description of an approaching time characterized by relief for all who were suffering:

> to give them a garland instead of ashes,
> the oil of gladness instead of mourning,
> the mantle of praise instead of a faint spirit.
> They will be called oaks of righteousness,
> the planting of the LORD, to display his glory.
>   (Isa. 61:3)

The third text is the centerpiece. As I pointed out in chapter 1, this is the Jubilee text itself, found in Leviticus 25 as part of the Holiness Code. The fifty-five verses of this chapter describe the Jubilee, "the year of the LORD's favor," to which scholars agree both Jesus and Isaiah were pointing when they proclaimed it and used that phrase. From their own religious heritage, with its centuries of Hebrew study of Torah, both Jesus and Isaiah knew of the continuing ideal of the Jubilee. They knew it too from the practice of the sabbatical year, when the Jews regularly rested the land. They knew it from the despised *prosboul*,[9] used by wealthy landowners to squirm their way out of Jubilee forgiveness of debt. They had learned that Jubilee was a heightened, holy time that began with the LORD speaking to Moses on Mount Sinai, and that it was described in Leviticus. In addition to Ringe, Trocmé, and Yoder, commentators such as J. Massyngbaerde Ford and J. A. Sanders agree that in the year 26, by citing Isaiah in that humble Nazareth synagogue, Jesus was declaring a Jubilee, just as the prophet had done in an earlier era.[10]

The preaching of Jesus at Nazareth and the traditions in Leviticus begin Jubilee at the same point: Sabbath. Jesus issues his proclamation on the Sabbath. And Leviticus 25 begins by drawing extraordinary and sustained attention to Sabbath, repeating the word (or its equivalent, the phrase "complete rest") six times in its initial verses. This Jubilee Sabbath is linked immediately to the land, and the word *land* is also used six times:

> When you enter the *land* that I am giving you, the *land* shall observe a *sabbath* for the LORD. Six years you shall sow your field, and six years you shall prune your vineyard . . . but in the seventh year there shall be a *sabbath* of *complete rest* for the *land,* a *sabbath* for the LORD: you shall not sow your field or prune your vineyard. You shall not reap the aftergrowth of your harvest or gather the grapes of your unpruned vine: it shall be a year of *complete rest* for the *land.* You may eat what the *land* yields during its *sabbath*—you, your male and female slaves, your hired and your bound laborers who live with you; for your livestock also, and for the wild animals in your *land* all its yield shall be for food.
> (Lev. 25:2b–7; italics added)

Only when this pattern of a yearlong Sabbath for the land—an agricultural fallow year—has become habitual does the Jubilee proper arrive, with the counsels to count off seven times seven years, sound the trumpet, hallow the fiftieth year, and proclaim liberty throughout the land to all its inhabitants.

We shall return to these latter verses in considering subsequent Jubilee traditions. As point of departure, however, the first seven verses of Leviticus prescribe a condition essential to the rest of Jubilee. If there is to be a year of the Lord's favor, and if people are to receive a garland instead of ashes, they must keep a yearlong period of complete rest, during which they let the land lie fallow. They must hallow the land so it will know the blessing of re-creation and so the poor might eat its yield. But they must also rest themselves, in order to listen to and answer the voice of their God.

Let the Land Lie Fallow:
A Twofold Meaning

As I indicated in the prelude to this chapter, the Jubilee instruction to let the land lie fallow has two distinct but related foci. The first is the land itself, the planet Earth that sustains us throughout life and receives us when we die. The second is the land, or to be more biblically true, the dust that is the physical core of human being—the "land" of our bodily reality.

The Land Itself

Leviticus 25 is unique among all the chapters of the Torah, because it is the only chapter that deals with the subject of land tenure in ancient Israel.[11] A "sabbath of the land" was probably observed during the preexilic period, even though we have no direct evidence of that from the time of the first temple. We do have ample evidence of an agricultural fallow year, however, from the period just before the common era. A report in 1 Macc. 6:49 and 53, for example, recalls that the city of Beth-zur had to surrender to the Syrians—the city lacked adequate provisions to endure the siege because the attack came in a sabbatical year. The historian Josephus also reports this incident along with other, similar examples. And Jubilee scholar Yoder comments that Jesus did not stress the agricultural fallow year in his Jubilee declaration at Nazareth because it was regularly practiced and people were familiar with it.

The teaching that the land itself must observe a sabbath to the Lord meant that every seventh year the soil was to be rested and planting, plowing, and harvesting were forbidden. During this seventh year, as the land lay fallow, no landowner could lay exclusive claim to anything growing on its own from the previous year. Instead, everyone was free to eat of the land, regardless of who owned the property.

This was in part an acknowledgment that the land deserved rest. But it was also a declaration that Yahweh was the ultimate owner of everything—a religious point—and that the natural growth of the land was intended to feed poor people and the nonhuman animals— a moral point. God promised enough food in the sixth year to carry the people through the seventh. As for the Jubilee, when it came to the great sabbatical of the forty-ninth year after "seven years of seven years," the length of that time period has two interpretations. Either, as the apocryphal book of Jubilees (written about 200 B.C.E.) says, the Jubilee year was one year long, extending from the start of the forty-ninth to the beginning of the fiftieth year, or, as Leviticus 25 indicates, it extended from the forty-ninth through the fifty-first years, making this Sabbath of Sabbaths a period lasting two full years.

In our time, Jubilee's provisions cannot always be followed completely or literally. Making fallow land available today can subject human beings to exhausted earth, disease from pesticides, even poisoning. Modern methods of agriculture often do not leave aftergrowth. And modern methods of food distribution—especially of excess food—are designed to make it available far more easily and quickly than by waiting for people to show up at the place it was harvested, hoping to find aftergrowth. In today's world, this Jubilee teaching usually needs contemporary, even metaphorical, interpretation.

Still, literal readings have their virtues. The Jubilee teaching that food which grows spontaneously is the property of all ought to be a religious and social principle that transcends politics throughout our world, where hunger and starvation continue to endanger entire peoples. The point is that although we cannot always follow the Jubilee particulars with exactness, the tradition as a whole is as relevant today as it was four thousand years ago. Jubilee is an ideal appropriate across the centuries.

It is also an ideal appropriate across widely varying cultures, many of which direct attention to attitudes of reverence, care for, and listening to the land. Not only are these attitudes found among the ancient Hebrews who gave us the Jubilee, they are also found among many of the world's peoples. These attitudes have special meaning for our own time, when the theme of connectedness with the earth has reappeared, although our era is not the one that "discovered" a spirituality of fallow land. At best, ours is a time of rediscovery and renewal.

In North America, an attitude of reverence for the land is closely associated with Native Americans. Squamish Chief Seattle reflected it in speaking about his people's relation to the land—and through it, to the Great Spirit. In the 1854 address he delivered on the occasion of the transferral of ancestral Indian lands to the U.S. federal government, he asked:

> How can you buy or sell the sky, the warmth of the land?
> If we do not own the freshness of the air and the sparkle
> of the water, how can you buy them? This we know. The
> earth does not belong to the humans; humans belong to
> the earth. This we know. All things are connected like the
> blood which unites one family. All things are connected.
> Whatever befalls the earth befalls the children of the earth.

The humans did not weave the web of life; they are merely
strands in it. Whatever they do to the web, they do to
themselves. . . . This earth is precious to God, and to harm
the earth is to heap contempt on its creator.[12]

One hundred and fifty years later, biblical scholar George Tinker points to similar attitudes in describing how Native Americans
read the Bible today and, in a reflection closely related to Jubilee's
teaching on fallow land, comments that his people's spiritual insights also begin with their relation to creation and the earth. He
describes the spirituality of Lakota and Dakota peoples as including a phrase in all their prayers that functions as "Amen" does in
other parts of Christianity. The phrase is *mitakuje oyasin,* and its
usual translation is "for all my relations." The phrase extends every
prayer outward in an ever-widening circle from the two-leggeds,
because each person who prays *mitakuje oyasin* knows that his or
her relatives necessarily include the four-leggeds, the winged ones,
the gilled ones, and all the living moving ones; they also include
trees, rocks, mountains, water, and land.[13]

Other peoples know these sacred relations too and resonate with
the disposition to let the land lie fallow. In a seventeenth-century Chi-
nese treatise on painting, called *The Mustard Seed Garden Manual,* the
artist is advised to compose his picture so that if, say, he is painting a
man looking at a mountain, the man will appear to be bent in an attitude of homage and the mountain will itself appear to be slightly
bent in an attitude of acknowledgment. Or if a lutist is playing her in-
strument under the moon, the painter is advised to make it appear
that the lutist is listening to the moon and the moon is listening to
her. The spiritual presupposition of this counsel is that humans stand
in a relation of reciprocity with the world and that like them, all of the
world is instinct with spirit and presence, the numinous and the sacred. As such, it must be treated with reverence and respect.[14]

Many in the human community are reclaiming such dispositions
today. The president of the Czech Republic, Václav Havel, gives two
further examples in speaking of the renewal of the lost integrity that
once existed as an ideal among all the orders of creation. His first
example is "an idea, perhaps as old as humanity itself, that we are
not at all just an accidental anomaly, the microscopic caprice of a
tiny particle whirling in the endless depths of the universe. Instead,
we are mysteriously connected to the universe, we are mirrored in
it, just as the entire evolution of the universe is mirrored in us."[15]

Havel's other example is the Gaia hypothesis, the theory that asserts we are parts of a greater whole. Named after an ancient goddess recognizable as an archetype of the Earth Mother in all religions, Gaia reminds us that our destiny is not dependent merely on what we do for ourselves. Our destiny is also dependent on what we do for Gaia. If we endanger her, we endanger life itself, for we are anchored in the earth and the universe. We are not here alone but are "an integral part of higher, mysterious entities against whom it is not advisable to blaspheme."[16] We must let Gaia lie fallow regularly, reverencing a nature that is never completely spent but is instead, as Gerard Manley Hopkins wrote, a "bent world" over which the Holy Ghost broods, "with warm breast and with ah! bright wings."[17]

The Human Land

Even as Jubilee teaches us to honor our relation to earth by letting it lie fallow and granting it a yearlong rest, there is another land to which we must attend and to which we must pay similar reverence. This is the land of ourselves, the tiny country each of us comprises, whose geography we know so well. We are to let that land, the land of our bodies, our blood, our breath, and our bones, lie fallow too. Regularly, we are to keep a sabbatical year—in ways we discover for ourselves—even as people do in academic life as part of their service and in religious ministry as part of their vocation. We can interpret the Sabbath command's direct reference to ourselves as, "*You* shall not plant or prune or produce. For you *also* are the earth." The Ash Wednesday ritual puts this to us directly, signing the human body with ashes and using the words of an ancient formula: "Memento, homo, quia pulvis es, et in pulverem reverteris." Remember, you who are human beings, that you are earth-dust—as well as star-dust—and one day you shall return to the physical universe to become its substance once again.

While *on* the earth, however, we need to remind ourselves that food from the land not only nourishes us, it becomes us. The wheat or the rice, the fruits or the vegetables that we eat daily become part of our substance. Such is the way of all living animals. "Let the land lie fallow" means let the land of ourselves be still periodically, giving it not only physical nourishment but regular, ritual rest.

Educationally and in terms of our spirituality, this teaching has many implications, most of them simple. Difficult, perhaps, but simple. We need to imitate the wise old woman who describes her life-music this way: "Sometimes ah' sets and thinks, and sometimes ah' jes' sets." We need to be people whose every activity has an underlying residue of receptivity, quiet, and contemplative being. We need to be listeners: not only to the creation surrounding us but to the creation and the land that we are, regularly praying that God will teach us to sit still. We need to attend to our pulse, our heartbeat, our respiration, and our daily rhythms, especially those of work and rest.

Furthermore, letting the land lie fallow provokes us to study the poetry of the scriptures with the attentiveness of a Hasidic rabbi, recalling Sholom Aleichem's Tevye, the milkman in *Fiddler on the Roof,* who wanted to be a rich man so he could sit for seven hours every day learning the power of the holy word: "Now that would be the sweetest thing of all." For some of us, practices such as these might even develop into our beginning and ending every day by setting aside time to follow our breath, repeating on each one as it enters and then flows forth: "Breathing in, I am inhaling Jubilee; breathing out, I am becoming Jubilee."

Such personal, individual breath then mingles with the breath of others with whom we share the planet. It mixes with the breath of the nonhuman animals, the sighs of the sky and the water creatures, and the whispering life forces within wood and dirt, flower and stone. It mingles with time as well, and with the rhythms of our own growth and decline, in the kind of connectedness Annie Dillard once described:

> I am a frayed and nibbled survivor in a fallen world, and I am getting along. I am aging and eaten and have done my share of eating too. I am not washed and beautiful, in control of a shining world in which everything fits, but instead am wandering awed about on a splintered wreck I've come to care for, whose gnawed trees breathe a delicate air, whose bloodied and scarred creatures are my dearest companions, and whose beauty beats and shines not *in* its imperfections but overwhelmingly in spite of them, under the wind-rent clouds, upstream and down.[18]

Sabbath

Jubilee teaching is clear about how we are to fulfill the command to let the land lie fallow: it is through the practice of Sabbath. What does it mean to live by Sabbath and as Sabbath? What does it mean to keep Sabbath? Any practicing Jew can give a far richer response to these questions than I. Nonetheless, thousands of years of practice emphasize the following:

> Sabbath means we live in *time,* in the *present.*
> Sabbath means we practice *shavat,* or *cessation:* it means we *stop.*
> Sabbath means we do these things in order to ready ourselves for *recreation in community.*

Sabbath Means We Live in Time

Essentially, Sabbath is a teaching about time and about dwelling in time. According to Rabbi Abraham Joshua Heschel, Sabbath is "like a palace in time with a kingdom for all. It is not a date but an atmosphere."[19] In Sabbath we try to become attuned to holiness in time.

One of the striking revelations of biblical teaching about Sabbath is the variety of sabbatical lengths. These include the weekly seventh-day Sabbath and the Day of Atonement Sabbath on the tenth day of the seventh month, both twenty-four hours long; the Sabbath of Pentecost, forty-eight hours long; the Sabbath of the seventh year, one year long; and the Sabbath of the Exile, seventy years long. Finally, the record cites the Sabbath of the Jubilee, the Sabbath of Sabbaths or Sabbath of Complete Rest that hallows the fiftieth year and extends as long as two full years.

Each of these describes Sabbath as a temporal reality. Yet each has a different duration, suggesting that Sabbath is not only the weekly twenty-four-hour-period most essential to its practice and most honored as its centerpiece. It can also be as brief as a three-minute pause when we catch our soul's breath or a half-hour prayer period every morning of our lives. It can be as extensive as a full year when we devote ourselves to study or the three-score-and-ten span that symbolizes an entire human life.

But from another temporal perspective, Sabbath describes more than a *length* of time; it also describes a discipline of *being* in time that enables us to listen for what we are called to do in time. As such, Sabbath acts as the reminder of the deeper dimension of all our time, the dimension of depth, when at every moment our choice as human beings is to live either superficially in time or profoundly in time. Sabbath acts as the religious summons to be present.

For human beings, the word *present* often refers either to an ephemeral moment in between past and future—the present—or to the physical presence in space acknowledged by the roll-call answer "Here." However, if these are the only meanings of human presence, time remains incomplete for us. This is because the fully human mode of presence is relationship-to-others: I can only say, "Here I am," with integrity when I have discovered myself in relation to you—and to everyone and everything else. To be incapable of presence is not only to be preoccupied but to be encumbered with ourselves.

Philosopher Gabriel Marcel, arguably the twentieth century's greatest philosopher of presence, writes that it is an undeniable fact of experience that some people offer us their presence; they are with us while others are not:

> Though it is hard to describe in intelligible terms, there are some people who reveal themselves as "present"—that is to say, at our disposal. . . . There is a way of listening which is a way of giving, and another way of listening which is a way of refusing, of refusing oneself; the material gift, the visible action, do not necessarily witness to presence. We must not speak of proof in this connection; the word would be out of place. Presence is something which reveals itself in a look, a smile, an intonation or a handshake.[20]

This common human experience can teach us that the opposite of being present in time is neither living in the past nor living in the future. The opposite of being present is being absent.

Drawing on his Japanese heritage, Kosuke Koyama captures the feeling of such presence. Writing about an experience he calls "Life Deepening," Koyama illuminates the relation between depth, time, and presence by observing that the care of Yahweh during forty years in the wilderness is a teaching about God's manner of presence. Koyama says God walks at the same speed persons walk, three miles an hour, and this image of the companionable, slowly moving, three-mile-an-hour God invites in the direction of depth rather than distance.[21] This deep presence is Sabbath's direction too.

However, the imagery of presence is not only about a divine way of being, it is about Divine Being itself. Writing of God as the "elusive" presence, Samuel Terrien develops this and makes presence essential theologically, saying that the motif of covenant is secondary in biblical theology, whereas the motif of presence is primary. This is because a covenant between God and humanity is possible only if Yahweh first chooses to be present to the chosen people; only a God who is there can make a covenant.[22] Then Terrien connects this God of presence to the creation of the Sabbath by saying that the Hebrews, aware of a God who was always in their midst, instituted Sabbath. When they did, Sabbath became not only the sacrament of their God; it became, and to this day remains, the sacrament of their God's *presence.*[23]

As a sacrament, Sabbath is the reminder that presence is God's way of being in our midst, our way of being with God, and the way in which we are with one another. Indeed, biblical religion, Jewish and Christian, conceives of spirituality—and its embodiment in prayer and in community and in ministry—as the *exercise* of the presence of God. This presence is awesome, thunderous, boring, occasionally ecstatic, regularly experienced as completely silent, and full of mystery. Often referred to as the Shekinah, this healing, shimmering presence of God is the core of an original experience that is still being articulated.

The New Testament records this experience of presence in connection with Jesus of Nazareth. Christian tradition describes the encounters the disciples had with him as a revelation of Emmanuel, "God with us." Their realization flowered only after the resurrection, as they knew him in the breaking of bread, and eventually flourished as the teaching that the Word of God, the divine Logos, had taken flesh and pitched its tent in their midst. At length the teaching became cemented, as the Gospel of Matthew records it, in the promise that this presence would last forever: "Remember, I am with you always." Like the early Hebrews, Jesus' disciples found a way to assert without equivocation that the mystery called God was present in the world, "to the end of the age" (Matt. 28:20).

Sabbath Means We Practice Shavat, or Cessation

In several Akkadian documents of ancient Mesopotamia, scholars have found the term *sabbatu,* which looks and sounds like the Hebrew word *sabbat.* Usually that word is translated as "day of rest for the heart."[24] For the Hebrews, however, the word from which Sabbath is derived is the verb *shavat,* which meant—and means—"to stop" and "to cease," with the noun translated as "cessation" or "desistance." Exodus 20:8–11 records this command as it first appeared:

> Remember the sabbath day, and keep it holy. Six days you shall labor and do all your work. But the seventh day is a sabbath to the LORD your God; you shall not do any work—you, your son or your daughter, your male or female slave, your livestock, or the alien resident in your towns. For in six days the LORD made heaven and earth, the sea, and all that is in them, but rested the seventh day; therefore the LORD blessed the sabbath day and consecrated it.

This creative cessation, this command to stop, is directed to work: in Walter Brueggemann's words, Sabbath is a "covenantal work stoppage."[25] Israel is to rest because God has also rested, since its God "is not a workaholic and has no need to be more secure, more sufficient, more in control or more noticed."[26] Nor do we. Ceasing labor is the way that human beings can carry out the first element in the Sabbath command: "Remember." Remember that God's world is not a place of endless productivity, ambition, or anxiety. Instead, it is a place where listening to and receiving word and world precede our tending to them.

Phrased and translated in the form of a negative injunction (You shall stop; You shall cease), the character of Sabbath is originally revealed as a mystical not-doing. When I first began teaching Sabbath to divinity students, many were intrigued and lured by its spirituality and desired it in their own lives. However, they often immediately equated this with practices of some kind and regularly came to me with paper and pencil asking, "What shall I *do* on Sabbath? What are the rules?"

There are, of course, practices associated with Sabbath—especially those of letting the land lie fallow and of recreation in community—but in general my response to the students was to hold that request at bay.[27] The first order of business (more accurately, of not-business) was to become adept at *not-doing*. Seen from one angle of vision, Sabbath is a "negative capability," a phrase poet John Keats used of Shakespeare to describe the capacity to live in uncertainty, mystery, stillness, even doubt, without irritably searching after facts and reasons. This is what I hoped would become for my students the basis of Sabbath in their lives, because that negative capability has an energy that moves naturally into rich, precise, and positive practice.

Rabbi Abraham Heschel goes even further than simple cessation of work. On the Sabbath, he says, Jews are to resist even the *thought* of work. To illustrate this, Heschel tells the story of a pious man who walks in his vineyard on the Sabbath and comes upon a fence with a breach that needs mending. "I shall fix that fence tomorrow," the man plans, "as soon as the Sabbath is over." But, Heschel continues, when he prepares to do this at the end of the Sabbath, he changes his mind. "Since I thought of mending it on the Sabbath," he decides, "I shall never repair it."[28] This suggests that on the Sabbath human beings ought not even think about labor.

The strictness and importance of the Sabbath command to stop, to cease work, and to not-do are borne out by the fact that its rigorous observance is enjoined in all of the biblical decalogues that constitute what is essential for covenant: Ex. 20:2–17; 20:23–24; 34:21; and Deut. 5:6–18. The utter seriousness of the Sabbath command reverberates centuries later—in Protestantism, in the form of restrictions in Puritan and Scottish Sabbath teaching, and in Catholicism, in the form of sanctions against absence from Sunday Eucharist that declared the absentee guilty of serious sin. Even when these commands seem overstrict, they nonetheless bear out the intuition that Sabbath must never be taken lightly.

But although it is a fundamental religious law, Sabbath cannot be made into the equivalent of restraints or blue laws. Instead, it is "a disciplined and regular withdrawal from the systems of productivity whereby the world uses people up to exhaustion. Sabbath is a daring recognition that, with the change in sovereigns from Pharaoh to Yahweh, unrewarded and unrewarding expenditure of labor is no longer required."[29]

This leads into the early conviction that despite being the ritually observed sacrament of God's presence, Sabbath was never entirely ceremonial; a conviction that also shapes the Jubilee. Instead, from early in its promulgation, Sabbath included the regular practice of justice. It was an ethical and moral teaching as well as a liturgical rite, a statement about human beings' relations with other humans (spouse, children, enslaved and indentured workers, strangers). It extended much further than the human community, however. Sabbath also assumed concern for other animals and the earth: the four-leggeds, the winged ones, the gilled ones once again. And only then, when the ceremonial and the ethical were in place, did the command to *stop* become transformed into the command to *rest*.

As such, Sabbath becomes a time for genuine listening and for the recollection in tranquillity that listening makes possible. As we welcome the Sabbath of full and complete rest, often referred to as "bride Sabbath," we can cultivate the second soul, or *neshamah yeterah,* given to everyone during it. We can become attentive to the suffering and the pain in the world; we can recognize the cloud and the logger and the logger's parents in the sheet of paper. And we can meditate on the implications in our own lives for what the rabbis refer to as the unity of devotion and deed; the marriage of what is real and what is to be realized; and the coming together of the world of mystery with the world of commandment.

In honoring rest, Sabbath cessation signals the very practical import of education to leisure. Leisure is closely allied to Sabbath and is itself often a form of silence. But it is the kind of silence that apprehends reality, the kind found in profound play and great art as well as in prayer. Actually, only those who are silent hear, and those who keep on talking do not hear. Sabbath rest reminds us that cultivating such leisured silence does not lead to "dumbness" or "noiselessness." Instead, as a restful waiting-on reality, it eventually impels us onto our knees in adoration and into the mystery-laden sunlit moments when our ordinary ways of doing are suspended and the ways of not-doing instruct us in welcoming Being itself. Encountering that Being then returns us, refreshed, to our world.

Sabbath Means Recreation in Community

The third facet of Sabbath is described by this ambiguous phrase where the first word means not only renewal of ourselves, as in *recreation,* but also the use of artistic imagination, as in *re-creation,* both of which occur in community. If they do not, the habits of presence and rest that Sabbath commands can turn us in on ourselves. They can make us even more individualistic than we are and shore up the too prevalent narcissism of the closing century.

Of recreation, both Jewish and Christian history make it clear that the Sabbath is to be accompanied by celebrative ceremony, festivity, and delight. Third Isaiah carries the injunction "Call the Sabbath a delight and the holy day of the LORD honorable" (58:13). One illuminating, although perhaps apocryphal, anecdote tells of the importance of Sabbath delight in the Judaism of the Middle Ages. Delight was so essential to Shabbat that if a person's joy was in fasting, then, despite the command to rejoice, that person was permitted to continue the fast even on the Sabbath. Its regulations were adjusted for the dyspeptic.

In 321 C.E., by which time Christians were honoring the first day as their Sabbath, the emperor Constantine proclaimed it a public holiday, and the magnificent liturgical developments of the fourth, fifth, and sixth centuries began, culminating in ceremonies that remain vibrant centerpieces of Eastern Christianity to this day. Throughout the rest of Christianity, artistic and aesthetic worship, festive dress, song, music, dance, and special food were the norm.

Too often, however, and periodically, Sabbath teaching manifested a troubling side. The evidence for this was a strange desire to control, to limit, and to put the lid on Sabbath joy. This occurred, for example, in the overly scrupulous rule-keeping of first-century Judea, which Jesus tried to break and break open not to destroy the Sabbath but to fulfill it. In more recent centuries, it was evident in commands to refrain from choices that might cause too much delight. For example, an eighteenth-century rule existed in one village in Scotland that said a rowboat was preferable to a sailboat on Sunday because the sailboat, although easier, might be more enjoyable.[30]

In the Christian churches, this troubling side was most evident in the separation of Sabbath practices from other acts of spirituality. Rather than a communal, ecclesial wholeness that integrated hallowing the time, gathering the people, probing the word, breaking the bread, and repairing the world, these works began to be seen as discrete practices, too often neither associated with daily life nor flowing from a living communion of many communities. In the original Sabbath commandment, ceremony and morality, liturgy and healing, contemplation and community are connected, and to this day the Jews do not separate them. But in too many Christian churches, although we have each of these, we do not have all of them as a mosaic where each coinheres within the others.[31] We are particularly poor, as people and as nations, at *Shabot shalom*—Sabbath peace.

In fact, it may be true to say that today the Christian religious world doesn't know what to do with Sabbath. My own conviction is that whenever we take part in a weakened or enfeebled Sabbath practice, "missing community" is the reason. The inability to engage in communal celebration with integrity and wholeness, not only in church or on Sunday but at home and at work and throughout the week, is a metaphor for disunity among ourselves—especially economic, educational, and racial disunity. These, in turn, symbolize the torn, rent body of the Christ; the disunity bred by centuries of church conflict that now appears even within individual communions. Even more tragic is the rupture between Christianity and Judaism, bred by centuries of the teaching of contempt as well as by the demonic anti-Semitism that culminated in the Holocaust.[32]

Perhaps the reason Sabbath recreation in our own communities does not occur is our continued separation from one another within and between the churches, our incomplete ecclesia, as well as our failure to acknowledge our Jewish roots, our Jewish blood, our Jewish sisters and brothers. It is difficult to encourage recreation in community if the paths to each other remain blocked. Here Sabbath reminds us that one of the fundamental meanings of sin is separation and sheds light on the impossibility of ever truly observing Sabbath unless the lion lies down with the lamb.

Despite such division, however, Sabbath remains a symbol and commandment not only of *recreation* in community but of *re-creation* in community. It remains a symbol and commandment of *tikkun olam*—the repair of the world. Lived to its fullest, Sabbath does not demand denial of activity but renewal of activity, directed toward new creation and toward re-creation. Such Sabbath re-creation is the work of Jubilee, with its traditions of forgiveness, freedom, and prophetic justice that eventually issue in still greater festivity, gratitude, and song.

Before we turn to these more active Jubilee works, however, we pause for the contemplation, cessation of work, and prayerful listening that is their necessary accompaniment. In this contemplation, cessation, and prayer, we begin to claim the vocation of Jubilee as we let the land lie fallow and grant it, as well as ourselves, a regular Sabbath. We savor the stillness and the solitude, knowing it is neither idleness nor laziness. Instead, it is the essential first step in becoming a Jubilee people in a world longing for a time of the Lord's favor.

For Further Reflection and Conversation

1. Where do you find the themes of liberation, connectedness, suffering, imagination, and repair of the world occurring in the teaching to let the land lie fallow?

2. Read Luke 4:16–20 and Isaiah 61:1–2. What clues do they offer to you concerning the meaning of Jubilee as a "year of the LORD's favor"?

3. Read Leviticus 25:1–7. What do the words *sabbath* and *complete rest* suggest to you?

4. How is a "Sabbath for the land" a part of your relation to the earth? What implications does this teaching have for education and for spirituality in the wider communities to which you belong?

5. What are some ways you might "exercise" the presence of God as an individual? As a member of a community or parish? As a citizen of the nation and the world?

6. When, where, how, and why are you called to *stop* and to *rest*?

7. In what ways might you support the wider community and society to engage in both meanings of recreation in community, that is, in *recreation* and in *re-creation*?

3

Forgiveness as a Way of Being in the World

Prelude

In her powerful account of a ministry that embraces both prisoners on death row and the families of crime victims, Helen Prejean relates an extraordinary conversation with the father of a seventeen-year-old boy who was senselessly murdered with his girlfriend by two brothers, Patrick and Eddie Sonnier. The father, Lloyd LeBlanc, told Prejean that he would have been content with imprisonment for Patrick, who received the death penalty. "Lloyd went to the execution, he says, not for revenge, but hoping for an apology," she remembers, "and Patrick Sonnier did not disappoint him. Before sitting in the electric chair he said, 'Mr. LeBlanc, I want to ask your forgiveness for what me and Eddie done.' Responding to him, Lloyd LeBlanc nodded his head, signaling a forgiveness he had already given."[1]

Forgiveness is the second Jubilee tradition. As I begin this chapter, probing what Jubilee contributes to the meaning of forgiveness, I offer Lloyd LeBlanc's story, asking readers to let it sit quietly in their souls as a guide, even a talisman, in taking up this theme.

I confess at the start of this chapter that I have borrowed from four authors, two of whom are essential to understanding Jubilee and two of whom are essential to understanding forgiveness. I have already noted the Jubilee scholars in passing, but here I single them out for their specific contributions. They are Sharon H. Ringe, who writes eloquently of *Jesus, Liberation and the Biblical Jubilee*, and

John Howard Yoder, himself dependent on André Trocmé, who writes passionately of *The Politics of Jesus*. The forgiveness scholars are Hannah Arendt in *The Human Condition* and Doris Donnelly in *Learning to Forgive*.[2] My debt to each of them will be obvious as the chapter proceeds.

To get at the fundamentals of Jubilee forgiveness, I have divided this chapter into two principal sections. The first includes words, phrases, and agents of forgiveness, each of which clarifies this Jubilee tradition. I see this section as a kind of primer that is at least partially a response to the question of the meaning of forgiveness. In the second section, I reflect on responses to three other questions—Forgive what? Forgive whom? and Forgive how?

A Forgiveness Primer: Key Terms

Forgiveness is an essential component of Jubilee. The particular form of forgiveness that Jubilee emphasizes is forgiveness from debt, and every commentator on the topic names it first. Jubilee forgiveness starts not with remission of "sin" or "trespass" or "wrong" but with the removal of the very specific burden of a monetary debt. Several words, appearing in both the Hebrew scriptures and the New Testament, are used to convey this initial understanding. *Deror,* for example, is the Hebrew word for "liberation," especially liberation from debt. Used only seven times in the Hebrew Bible, it refers to the Jubilee every time it appears.[3]

Other terms share an etymology. Among these are *aphiēmi,* meaning to remit, release from debt, send away; it is a Greek term that also shows up as the noun *aphesis* and, in the Septuagint, as *aphiēnai.*[4] These words are important because they begin as references to remission or release or dismissal—liberation—from obligations tied to legal requirements, bonds, and debts (especially financial ones). However, they can also refer to forgiveness in the more usual religious, ethical, and moral sense: as the removal of and atonement for sin.

Commenting on Jesus' insistence on the necessity of forgiveness—what in this chapter I call forgiveness as a way of being in the world—Hannah Arendt points out two additional terms that develop understanding of forgiveness further. Along with *aphiēnai,* she writes that when Jesus says you shall forgive even if someone sins against you seven times a day and subsequently turns to you again seven times saying, "I repent," such a turning may also be an example of *metanoein*, meaning a change of mind, a *re*-turning, a tracing back of our steps—what Jews call *teshuvah*.[5] But forgiveness here is also directed toward *hamartanein*, interpreted and translated as "trespassing," which means missing the mark, failing, and going astray.

I take the time for this primer because when we come to the Lord's Prayer and pray "forgive us our debts as we forgive our debtors," the word for debts is *opheilēma*, which signifies precisely a monetary debt. Some commentators—Yoder, for example—noting "debts" as the correct translation, say those who use "trespasses" are wrong.[6] And Rosemary Radford Ruether reminds her readers that in the Lord's Prayer, "debt" has often been spiritualized and privatized by the substitution of "sins" or "wrongs" or, notably, "trespasses."[7] Both of these are important and significant cautions.

Still, if we are among those who pray "forgive us our trespasses as we forgive those who trespass against us," in addition to "forgive us our debts," my own conviction is that although that may be an incorrect and inaccurate translation, it is not *necessarily* wrong. The long experience of Christian tradition links us to all who have prayed it in the centuries preceding us; the phrase also links us to the practice of forgiveness as a central element in religious life. While remembering that Jesus makes forgiveness of debts the essential forgiveness component of Jubilee, the long history of the church calls attention to other forms of forgiveness also necessary for Jubilee people. In this chapter I ask the reader to consider the proposition that given a developed and contemporary understanding of the Jubilee, every time we ask for forgiveness praying both "forgive us our trespasses as we forgive those who trespass against us" and "forgive us our debts as we forgive our debtors"—holding onto both is a wise move—we act as jubilarians, since in all its renderings the Our Father is a jubilary prayer.

Returning to Leviticus 25, I would also point out that the source of Jubilee instruction on forgiveness is connection to the land and to the command to let the land lie fallow. As the psalmist knew, "The earth is the LORD's and all that is in it, the world, and those who live in it" (Ps. 24:1). And, according to Lev. 25:23–38, when the Jubilee year comes, even if it has been necessary to give up your land because of debt, your right to redeem it is at last approved. If you have indentured yourself to pay off a debt, you are forgiven and released from those debts. And if, as a parent, you have sold your child for a stipulated sum and a specified number of years, you are released, as are your children—a situation that is starkly real today for those desperately poor parents in Southeast Asia and elsewhere who regularly sell their children into prostitution or forced labor. When the Jubilee comes, says Lev. 25:54, "they and their children with them shall go free."

The Forgivers

Reflection on those who demonstrate forgiveness is an additional way to understand Jubilee forgiveness. The idea that forgiveness is a religious, even theological, quality immediately ties it to God, suggesting it as a divine power. In the New Testament and in subsequent Christian theology, the God and Father of Jesus especially is constantly described as one who forgives, although forgiveness does not belong only to the God of the Christians. None of us ought leave out the Allah who listens to the prayers of Allah's children or the Yahweh who washes sins that are as red as scarlet and makes them as white as snow.

Mythically, forgiveness can even be imagined as what Joseph Campbell refers to as a "mask of God." Something serves as such a mask if it inspires awe, situates us in the cosmos, locates us socially in relation to one another, and interprets for us who we are psychologically. Whenever forgiveness awes us, or helps us know our place in creation, or connects us to one another, or interprets us to ourselves, we are meeting God, wearing one of the divine masks.[8] It is a God who grants forgiveness in relation to the way *we* grant forgiveness and whose inner being (if one can speak of God's psychology) is not only to grant but to *be* forgiveness.

God, however, is not the only one who forgives. In a striking and in other ways damning passage, Hannah Arendt—a Jew writing after the Holocaust—directs attention to Jesus' forgiveness. She reflects on how relatively recent forgiveness is in human affairs. In doing so, she lifts up the reemerging sense of religious vocation that is one of this century's challenges to Jubilee, stressing forgiveness as social and political, not simply personal or interpersonal. Arendt writes that Jesus of Nazareth was the one who discovered the role of forgiveness in human affairs. And even though Jesus made this discovery in a religious context and used religious language to articulate it, she argues that is no reason for humanity to take it any less seriously than might be the case if it were a more secular discovery. She laments the element in political philosophy that has tended to exclude such religious insights from authentic political life.[9]

Then Arendt continues, offering a conclusion in harmony with the dream of creating a Jubilee world that includes the practice of forgiveness:

> Certain aspects of the teaching of Jesus of Nazareth which are not primarily related to the Christian religious message but sprang from experiences in the small and closely knit community of his followers, bent on challenging the public authorities in Israel, certainly belong [here] even though they have been neglected because of their allegedly exclusively religious nature. The only rudimentary sign of an awareness that forgiveness may be the necessary corrective for the inevitable damages resulting from action may be seen in the Roman principle to spare the vanquished (*parcere subiectis*)—a wisdom entirely unknown to the Greeks—or in the right to commute the death sentence, probably also of Roman origin, which is the prerogative of nearly all Western heads of state.[10]

We human beings have the power of forgiveness too. Not only does God forgive through us, making forgiveness a primordial sacramental act. Not only does Jesus preach forgiveness, making it a centerpiece of his gospel. We who are *imago Dei*, the image of God, also possess the power to forgive. To return to Hannah Arendt once more, it is critical to realize that had we not the power to forgive one another, we would be unable to undo the wrong we have done. "Without being forgiven, released from the consequences of our actions, our capacity to act would be confined to one single deed from which we could never recover; we would remain the victims of its consequences forever."[11] Arendt compares that situation to being like the sorcerer's apprentice who lacked the magic formula to break the spell.

The paradox here is that we cannot forgive ourselves. All of us stuck here together must try to get along; all of us must learn the route of mutual forgiveness. Essential to creating a Jubilee world, forgiving and being forgiven are part of the human situation, a "necessary corrective" to evil, and part of the connectedness that illuminates a common destiny. "There is no sin, not even the most intimate and secret one, the most strictly individual one, that exclusively concerns the person committing it. With greater or lesser violence, with greater or lesser harm, every sin has repercussions on the . . . whole human family."[12] That statement might have come from Thich Nhat Hanh or Mohandas Gandhi. Actually, it comes from John Paul II and fosters the correlative: every act of forgiveness also has repercussions on the whole human family.

Further, if we do not forgive what lies in our power to forgive, we keep alive the quid pro quo equation of returning evil for evil. With forgiveness, however, we create the possibility of an end to violence. Exercising it, we may even demonstrate the presence of grace as one outcome of our personal, social, and political acts of forgiveness.

Finally, the practice of forgiveness can become a liberating kind of forgetting. At the very least it can be an opportunity for getting over the encounter with evil—our own and others'—and getting on with life. This is a getting over and getting on learned from the forgetting action that human beings commonly assume in God when asking divine forgiveness but rooted too in the recognition that the *amnesty* which is one of the first signs of Jubilee forgiveness has the same root as *amnesia.* The following story told by Elaine Roulet (who, like Helen Prejean, is in prison ministry) illustrates this mysterious, forgetting forgiveness:

> There once lived a wise woman, and it was clear to all who knew her that God spoke to her, and she spoke to God. But she was a concern, and if the entire truth is told, a thorn in the side of the local bishop, who tried to think of ways to reduce her power.
>
> One day, believing he had discovered how to do this, he came to her and said, "Wise woman, I have heard that God speaks to you and you speak to God. I want you to prove it by asking God to reveal to you my innermost sins"—for being a bishop, he had many.
>
> The wise woman agreed that she would, since she did indeed speak to God, and God did indeed speak to her. So on a day agreed upon for the wise woman to carry back God's response, the bishop returned to hear it. He asked the wise woman whether she had petitioned God for the names of his innermost sins. She replied that she had, and so the bishop asked her the further question, "What did God say?"

Her answer was immediate. "God said, 'The bishop's innermost sins? I'm sorry. Tell the bishop I forgot.'"[13]

Fundamental Questions

Having taken time to explore the roots and the *nature* of Jubilee forgiveness, the first fundamental question in terms of its *practice* is "Forgive what?" This question needs to be elaborated immediately, so that it is clear that Jubilee people are called both to *grant* forgiveness and to *request* and *receive* it, whether that occurs for them as individual persons, as families, as communities, as nations. "Forgive what?" is actually shorthand for "And be forgiven of what, ask forgiveness for what?" even as the next question, "Forgive whom?" includes "And be forgiven by whom, ask forgiveness of whom?" and the final question, "Forgive how?" includes "And be forgiven in what ways?" That said, the responses to "Forgive what?" are that we must forgive everything—or at least, everything we can. We must forgive debts; we must forgive sins and trespasses; and we must forgive omissions.

Forgive What?

Forgive Everything We Can

As human beings, we are called to forgive everything that it is in our power to forgive. Arendt names as the exception those things we are unable to punish, saying, "It is quite significant, a structural element in the realm of human affairs, that human beings are unable to forgive what we cannot punish and unable to punish what has turned out to be unforgivable."[14] She uses the phrase "radical evil" to refer to those atrocities that sometimes are understood as literally crying to heaven, not to earth, for vengeance; those deeds that "dispossess us of all power." These are the offenses Jesus was referring to in saying of those responsible for them that it would be better that a millstone be hung around their necks and that they be cast into the sea.

What guidance can a community offer to those who cannot forgive everything—or everyone: the human beings who conceived of and built Auschwitz and Birkenau, of whom Elie Wiesel said fifty years later, "Although we know that God is merciful, please God, do not have mercy for those people who created this place";[15] the rapists who have too often ruined an individual's entire life and that of her family and sometimes her nation; the torturers of children during the Cambodian genocide, who created unspeakably cruel devices designed to force young children to mutilate and kill one another;[16] the exterminators of entire tribes of native peoples in North America? We return to this issue below, but among the responses to an appeal for guidance is that forgiveness may sometimes occur only after an appeal for it on the part of the evildoers, and only after a long period of time. Conceivably, and upon their request, a community may forgive or withhold forgiveness in the name of individuals who are its members, for whom the burden of forgiving particular acts of evil is too close and too heavy and often an experience of violation. There are circumstances, however, where forgiveness is not possible, and its disposition must be left to God.[17]

Forgive Debts

Even as some sin may escape forgiveness, so may some debts. It is unrealistic to assume this Jubilee prescription is true for college loans, for example, which can be paid back once a person is earning, although for those overwhelmed by such debt, the request for forgiveness may be worth trying. More likely, the recipient who is now the debtor may have to work off the debt during an agreed-upon period of service.

An easier situation may be debts owed to us by family members—the brother-in-law who borrowed seven hundred dollars in 1966 for a new car and still hasn't paid us back should be forgiven, not so much for his sake as for ours. Hanging onto resentment for many years over this or similar unpaid debts probably does more violence to the lender than the borrower and is certainly not in the spirit of Jubilee forgiveness.

The debts that should draw our attention, however (especially if we are in the 20 percent of the world's peoples who hold 83 percent of its wealth while the poorest 20 percent receive 1.4 percent of its total income), are those stemming from loans made available years ago to so-called developing nations in Asia, Africa, and Latin America, where the compound interest on the loans is now so great that the poorer nations are unable to get out from under the resulting burden. While it may be relatively easy to forgive a brother-in-law, many still find it difficult to grant the forgiveness demanded by global sin and global debt; we may even find it difficult to accept the teaching that affluent nations owe it to poorer nations to forgive them their debts, and if they do not, they cannot be forgiven either.

Corporate or global sin exists in many guises. An example is the World Bank's insistence on "policies of 'structural adjustment' that demand that poor, indebted nations cut back on their development of jobs, education, health and welfare for their people in order to subordinate their economies to the one goal of producing exports to repay the debt."[18] A colleague who recently returned to New York after visiting Guyana and Surinam reminded me that 60 percent of each of those countries' monetary resources go into payment of such debt. They are but two of the countries that are being destroyed by the weight of this burden, and those of us in a position to remove this debt and who fail to do so are contributing—financially—to the poverty and the deaths of their people.

In such circumstances, the Jubilee tradition of forgiveness, primarily of debt, could not be more relevant and more applicable today. It is difficult to know how land may be returned in all circumstances—we need think only of the death and destruction in Bosnia-Herzegovina, Chechnya, and Israel/Palestine—although the kind of steps taken in South Africa in this decade, the redress offered by affirmative action for both African American and Native American citizens in this century, and the willingness to negotiate the Mexican debt by the United States are seedbeds of further action.

At the very least, however, all religious people of goodwill ought to take on responsibility for petitioning both the World Bank and the United States government to erase those foreign debts that are crushing our hemispheric neighbors. Local parishes and congregations ought to work with at least two communities poorer than themselves, one in this country and one beyond its borders. And each of the years leading up to the Jubilee year 2000 and following it in the new century must be considered an occasion to declare a Jubilee when not only the land lies fallow but all debts that can be remitted, are.

Forgive Sins and Trespasses

The words *sins* and *trespasses* here include those we are aware of but also those we don't know or can't figure out how to forgive or how to ask forgiveness for. I think, for example, of a friend—a clinical psychologist—whose work brings her into contact with prison personnel who have responsibility for executions in a federal prison where she works. Regularly, they come for counseling and describe not only their belief they have done wrong but the physical symptoms of their bodies' corroboration of that belief. They often experience great trauma because they have participated in something that is evil and must be forgiven, although their state and their nation tell them there is nothing to forgive, and we, their fellow citizens, silently support their killing in our name.

This is a case where people *experience* their own actions as wrong. The opposite can happen too: sometimes people eventually realize that conduct they have identified as wrong is actually not sinful at all. Such was the case in feminist Valerie Saiving's conclusion that women's sins were not usually pride, self-love, and will-to-power, which many Christian ethicists had taught was the meaning of sin. Instead, women's sins were far more likely to be triviality, diffuseness, dependence on others for self-definition, and refusal to name oneself.[19]

Similarly, small children sometimes believe they have committed sin by saying the *f* word or the *s* word or the *d* word or by finding themselves punished for what is a normal and healthy sexual curiosity. One of playwright Brian Friel's most poignant stories, "The First of My Sins," is a seven-year-old boy's account of his dawning awareness of what actually is sin in his life. Although his mother continually reminds him that in his first confession he must tell the priest he has tormented his older sister, punched his friends, and tried to find out the color of an older neighbor's knickers, the child feels no guilt for any of these. Instead, he recognizes that in sharing a secret not his to tell—his knowledge of a long-ago theft committed by an uncle who lives with his family—he has been responsible for great harm. His uncle is dismissed from the household, and the boy knows he has sinned—though not in the ways his mother would name—and needs to be forgiven.[20]

Forgive Omissions

One catechetical teaching on sin names it as "any willful thought, word, deed, or *omission* against the law of God." Omission refers here to offenses we commit by leaving things out, ignoring what needs to be done, or not noticing what we have done and how we

might unthinkingly harm others. It is an arena tied to Vincent de
Paul's counsel "Pray that the poor forgive you your charity to
them." The offenses here are not so much in the area of guilt as of
responsibility and are tied to the notion of privilege.

In chapter 1, I drew on a comment by Judith Plaskow that a vital spirituality will be mystical as well as political, although those
with a political spirituality are often unaware of their own privilege
and those with a mystical spirituality are often unaware of a social
world. The same comment may be used about our omissions. We
may need forgiveness not only for what we have done but also, as
the prayer for forgiveness in the Christian liturgy names it, "for
what we have failed to do." I suspect that what we fail to do—our
omissions—regularly arises from our unawareness of our privilege,
whether that is racial privilege, gender privilege, economic privilege, educational privilege, or even—when it comes to our relation
with children—grown-up privilege. On this theme, Peggy McIntosh's forty-six examples of the privilege she enjoys because she is
white—"I can go shopping alone most of the time, fairly well assured that I will not be followed or harassed by store detectives"; "I
can be sure that my children will be given curriculum materials that
testify to the existence of their race"; "I am never asked to speak for
all the people of my racial group"—are a pertinent examination of
conscience.[21] They can move us to request forgiveness for the privilege we unwittingly assume as ours. Such privilege routinely
blinds us to the works of justice our privilege demands, works we
too often omit from our lives.

Forgive Whom?

The next fundamental question is "Forgive (and be forgiven by)
whom?" The answers: our families; those with a family-like or intimate connection to us; the people our people have harmed; those
whose sin against us is so great it is impossible to forgive; and, on
occasion, ourselves.

Our Families

For many people, family forgiveness is often the most difficult:
forgiveness of our parents, siblings, spouses, former spouses, adult
children, especially if the sin was committed by more powerful persons toward those they should have been protecting. Family forgiveness is also difficult because no one can hurt us more than
those we have known from the earliest years of our lives.

The story of Joseph found in Genesis is an apt illustration of family sin and family forgiveness. In *How God Fix Jonah,* Lorenz Graham uses a West African version of English to tell the story of the dramatic moment when Joseph speaks his forgiveness. Arguably, of course, he had cause to ask forgiveness himself when he was younger, especially for his self-importance, his pride, and his insensitive and big-mouth thoughtlessness in recounting his dreams of superiority to his brothers. However, his brothers' actions in selling him into slavery were a punishment that hardly fit those offenses.

Now, however, it is decades later, and the brothers, released from famine by traveling to Egypt, are returning home to Canaan. It is the moment after the discovery in their possession of Joseph's silver cup, which they are accused of stealing:

> The brothers fear and beg
> And Joseph's heart grow big inside
> He send all other people out
> And he cry small.

> The brothers look and wonder
> But Joseph call each one by name
> and then he say in Canaan talk, "This man Joseph be
>   you brother."

> The brothers no can speak
> They no can see the place they be
> They see rice farm in Canaan land
> And Joseph's bundle like a king
> They see Mandingo traders with a slave
> And Old Man Jacob with a coat
> But Joseph softly, softly say "Nev mind. God's hand
>   done fix the thing."[22]

Here is one word of family forgiveness. "Nev mind. God's hand done fix the thing."

Our Intimates

We must also forgive those who have a family-like, personal, or intimate connectedness to our lives. Here is a case where those offending generally must recognize the harm they are doing and ask for forgiveness first. An example is found in the diaries of Oscar

Romero, where the soon-to-be-martyred archbishop describes the pain he experiences from his brother bishops. Reflecting on a meeting with some of them, he notes:

> I was subjected to many false accusations by the other bishops. I was told that my preaching is subversive and violent; that my priests provoke a climate of violence among the peasants; and that we should not complain about the abuses that the authorities are committing. . . . It has been a bitter day because of this event and I lament that the divisions among the bishops will be worsened.[23]

On another occasion, when it appears to Romero that the papal nuncio is shunning him, he writes:

> I noted in the bishops the same desire to marginalize me. The people, on the other hand, gave me a warm ovation when I left the church. . . . I do not feel any vanity but rather joy in my harmony with the people who expect from their prophets and pastors an increasingly deep solidarity.[24]

And two weeks before his murder, he writes:

> I fear, given the aggressiveness with which [two of the bishops] attacked me, that we have not achieved much with respect to deep feelings of unity. The Lord will judge. On my part, I want to offer up all these sacrifices, and all this unpleasantness so that the gospel may triumph and that we may all be converted to the truth and to the service of God and our people.[25]

One can only imagine Romero's pain that the attacks came from those who were so close; one can only hope that those who inflicted the pain eventually repented and sought forgiveness.

Those People Our People Have Harmed

In many cases, we *must* ask for forgiveness—in word or deed—before it can be granted to us or felt by us. This is particularly true in a third instance: forgiveness sought from those people whom our people have harmed. Word and deed are both evident in an experience described by Regina Coll of the University of Notre Dame.

Regina, a white woman, is a member of an African American Catholic parish known for its extraordinarily moving liturgies. On Holy Thursday, just before Easter, in preparing for the foot-washing, the pastor asked Regina if she would be one of the first twelve to let him wash her feet, to help start off the rest of the congregation in joining in the mandatum and becoming part of the ritual.

She agreed, and when the appointed time came, the pastor knelt before her, washed her feet, and then—as he was drying them—paused and spoke to her with words not in the official rubrics. "Regina," he said, "I am so sorry for what too many of those of us who are men in our church are doing to too many of you who are women. I ask your forgiveness."

Moved by his words—as well as by his deed—Regina's "tears were full of eyes" (to draw on a phrase of e. e. cummings).[26] But then she saw a woman waiting to have her feet washed and realized what she might do. She asked the woman to let her wash her feet, and the woman agreed. As Regina dried them, she too paused and spoke words not in the official rubrics. "I am so sorry," she said, "for what too many of us who are white have done and continue to do to those of you who are black. I ask your forgiveness."

The forgiveness the African American woman signaled did not surprise Regina. In a symbolic, sacramental response to the racism of which Regina spoke, she nodded her forgiveness as so many other black women have done. Like Alice Walker, who has named the danger of a refusal to forgive racism directed against her as being "a stone; a knot in my psychic system,"[27] that woman acknowledged that when repentance is genuine, the refusal to forgive can often do harm to an already bruised spirit.

For U.S. Americans seeking to live the Jubilee, this is a reminder of the great national sin of our country's white people: our racism. It is a racism familiar to the Nisei—the Japanese Americans interned in their own country during World War II—of whom the U.S. government asked partial forgiveness fifty years later in the form of monetary grants. It is a reminder of forgiveness still needing expression to the peoples of Hiroshima and Nagasaki by the United States as the fiftieth anniversary of those cities' destruction has come and gone. Most of all, it is a reminder that forgiveness has not yet been sought by many of the nonblack majority in this nation from the descendants of African peoples who first reached U.S. shores almost four hundred years ago.[28]

The Impossible to Forgive

A fourth category includes those who have been sinned against so greatly it seems impossible to forgive, who yet find themselves impelled to grant it. Lloyd LeBlanc, quoted in the prelude to this chapter, is one example. Corrie ten Boom is another. After she was released from the camp where her sister Betsie died during the Nazi Holocaust, she lectured and preached on the need to forgive enemies. One evening she was greeted after her lecture by a man she recognized as the SS guard at the shower room in the processing center at Ravensbruck:

> "How grateful I am for your message, Fraulein," he said. "To think that, as you say, He has washed my sins away!"
>
> And suddenly, it was all there—the roomful of mocking men, the heaps of clothing, Betsie's pain-blanched face.
>
> His hand was thrust out to shake mine. And I, who had preached so often to the people in Bloemendaal the need to forgive, kept my hand at my side.
>
> Even as the angry, vengeful thoughts boiled through me, I saw the sin of them. Jesus Christ had died for this man; was I going to ask for more? Lord Jesus, I prayed, forgive me and help me to forgive him.
>
> I tried to smile. I struggled to raise my hand. I could not. I felt nothing, not the slightest spark of warmth or charity. And so again I breathed a silent prayer. Jesus I cannot forgive him. Give me your forgiveness.
>
> As I took his hand a most incredible thing happened. From my shoulder along my arm and through my hand a current seemed to pass from me to him, while into my heart sprang a love for this stranger that almost overwhelmed me.
>
> And so I discovered that it is not on our forgiveness any more than on our goodness that the world's healing hinges but on His. When He tells us to love our enemies, He gives, along with the command, the love itself.[29]

Ourselves

In most cases, we cannot forgive ourselves for what we have done to others; that is their prerogative, not ours, and in most cases, forgiving ourselves is both facile and misplaced action. Still, there are circumstances where we must let go of self-condemnation and get on with our lives, especially when we have received the grace to think of ourselves as sinners. We probably need to forgive ourselves our tempers, our addictions, our vanities, our arrogance, our smugness, our failure to do what we must and be who we are, of-

ten as much as the proverbial seventy-times-seven times. I am reminded of a TV reporter who, standing at the door of a busy AIDS
ward in San Francisco, finished his interview with this one last
question: "Is there anything else I ought to say to viewers?"

The nurse who had guided him through the ward thought for a
moment and then realized there was one thing. "Yes," she replied
softly, reflecting on what she had learned in her work. "Tell them
to forgive themselves; tell them especially, in their eternal pursuit
of youth, to forgive themselves for growing old. It is a privilege de-
nied to so many."

Forgive (and Be Forgiven) How?

When We Are Ready

Sometimes forgiveness—and the acknowledgment of wrong—
takes a long, long time. It was a remarkable experience for me, de-
livering the Tuohy lectures and writing this text in 1994 and 1995,
to see this temporal dynamic played out on the world stage. Beginning in June of 1994 with the commemoration of D Day, the
world news has included daily expressions of remembrance, remorse, and request for forgiveness among the warring parties of
World War II. "Japan Offers Aid to Atone for 'Comfort Women' "
read a headline from Manila in August 1994; "I ask for forgiveness
for what Germans did to you," said Germany's president, Roman
Herzog, to Polish Jews on the fiftieth anniversary of the uprising in
the Warsaw ghetto; "Lithuanian Asks Remorse for Crimes against
Jews," is another headline, coming from Vilnius. Emperor Akhito
of Japan stopped at Pearl Harbor after a state reception in the
United States, although he was only a little boy in 1941. And in
February 1995, two essayists finally turned attention on ordinary
Germans as victims during the war: "In this bloody century, Germans have sinned more than they have been sinned against. Thus
none of the many 50th-anniversary observances have marked Ger-
man victimhood. Until now." Then the writers, Christian Habbe of
Germany's *Der Spiegel* and Donald Koblitz of the U.S. State Department, recall in terrible detail the firebombing of Dresden, a city
with no military targets, chosen for firebombing by British and U.S.
air forces largely because it was still intact—a decision insanely
reminiscent of Dr. Strangelove. And because the Holocaust was
such an unthinkable horror and the Nazi dictatorship so uniquely

evil, the calculated firebombing of more than half a million de-
fenseless civilians in the dying days of the war has been little recognized. But the firebombing, say these two men, was "a sin that
was visited on Dresden," and people have begun to speak openly
about this sin—this moral outrage—and to ask why it hap-
pened.[30]

I find all of these accounts remarkable for their Jubilee connection, occurring as they do in the forty-ninth and fiftieth years
after what are global, planetary sins. But I also find them instructive of the temporal nature of forgiveness, especially when,
as in the cases of the dismantling of the Smithsonian exhibit
lamenting the use of the atomic bomb and the return of veterans
to Iwo Jima, the time for forgiveness had not yet arrived. Often
the coalescing of circumstances that mark the time as "now"
takes a long, long time. Forgiveness comes only when there is
readiness, and often only when there is genuine repentance on
the part of the one sinning.

The caution for personal relations is that we may not have fifty
years, either to repent or to grant forgiveness. Therefore, to echo
one victim speaking to the one who was to betray him, "Do quickly
what you are going to do" (John 13:27b).[31]

By Returning and by Pilgrimage

Ten years ago I made a first visit to Dachau. I prepared in silence
and prayer by studying, memorizing, and then repeating the Shema
as a mantra the entire time, so that I might bring a discipline of
mourning to my pilgrimage. I was troubled with visiting Germany:
since my childhood I had associated it with the blood of martyrs
and with what a nation had done to people it thought different. But
when I walked through the camp—it was snowing and it was
cold—and paused at the memorials, the crematorium, and the lone
barracks still standing, the returning itself taught me something
new. Halfway through that visit the recognition reached me: "This
is not only about the Nazis, Maria; it's about *you*. It's about the evil
of which you are capable, even as it is about the evil you have already done."

I found similar education by returning to Hiroshima and walking through the Peace Park surrounded by hundreds of Japanese
schoolchildren. I found it, too, by walking into the bombed shell of
the old Coventry Cathedral, destroyed in 1942. Both of the latter

pilgrimages, in each case to a place that was rebuilt, shining and new, offered me images of death and resurrection.

I believe the same experience touches those who stand on the borders of Central American countries as witnesses for peace. But one's returning need not involve travel abroad. It is as available as the nearest shelter for battered women or soup kitchen for those who are homeless. Our *teshuvah* to these places is also a request for forgiveness: for our complacency, for our acceptance of unequal distribution of resources throughout the world, for neglect of our universal sisterhood and brotherhood with one another.

By Ritual

One of the best known contemporary, corporate rituals of repentance in religious circles is the yearly Yom Ha'Shoah commemoration practiced not only by Jews but by many Christian denominations who have placed it in their lectionaries. Ritual prayer for forgiveness is as old as religion itself: the scapegoat sent into the desert; the smearing of ashes on the forehead at the beginning of Lent and the ecclesial season of Lent itself; the sacrament of reconciliation; the burning of symbols from the past.

Equally well known are family practices and family prayer at the end of the day, with siblings and spouses learning never to go to bed angry with one another or without asking forgiveness.

Each of these rituals regularly has two critical elements. The first is a meditative listening, where we let the land lie fallow and attend quietly to what is within. Psychotherapist Estelle Frankel describes a meditation she leads in preparation for Yom Kippur, the holiest day of the year in the Jewish cycle of time. The meditation has the power to heal and to bring about atonement.

> Before starting the meditation I spend five minutes guiding people into a relaxed state of mind. Then I suggest that they focus on something about themselves or something that happened in their lives that they have had difficulty accepting or reconciling with. After they get in touch with that memory, I ask them to find the ways in which that very thing has also empowered or blessed them in some way. When people are able to connect their painful memories or experiences with some redeeming outcome they frequently experience a deep sense of forgiveness and peace.[32]

A second element often present in rituals of forgiveness is mourning, variously expressed throughout the world as keening, wailing, screaming, or raging. The tears held in as a result of sin, trespassing, or debt can become a kind of ice, shutting us down interiorly. Once melted, they make the heart and the spirit moist and often release a person from sin through the surround of ritual words, actions, and processes.

By Following the Process of Maimonides

Maimonides was a medieval philosopher and codifier of Jewish law who outlined the stages of *teshuvah,* or "turning" (in the sense of conversion and forgiveness). His teaching is found in the *Mishnah Torah* and the process has five steps, which are as follows:

> awareness—*hakarat ha'chet,* where *chet* means "missing the mark" or "sin";
> verbal confession—*vidui;*
> regret—*charatah;*
> resolve—to make amends, to straighten out what we've twisted or broken;
> resistance—the refusal to repeat the actions for which we are seeking forgiveness.[33]

As a Catholic Christian of a certain age, I recognized this teaching immediately when I first encountered it, for it corresponds with the sacramental practice of the Roman Catholic church that I grew up in. Forgiveness involves the awareness of sin that comes from an examination of conscience; the verbal practice of confession, generally to someone else in the community; sorrow for sin, the regret of *charatah;* making amends through accepting works of penance and repentance; and the firm purpose to resist repeating the offense, or as Jesus of Nazareth counseled, the intention to leave the place of temptation—wherever the place may be—and sin no more.

We Practice Forgiveness as a Difficult, Daily, Lifelong Struggle

This is the last response I want to make to the question "Forgive—and be forgiven—how?"; for forgiveness is rarely easy, and its burden and weight can surprise us at unexpected moments when we have momentarily forgotten its price. Because he understands this so well, I return to Lloyd LeBlanc, with whose story I began this chapter. He says that on the night his son was killed, he arrived with sheriff's deputies and walked through the cane field where the bodies lay, in order to identify his son. He knelt by the seventeen-year-old body, "down there with his two little eyes sticking out like bullets," and prayed the Our Father. And when he came to the words "Forgive us our trespasses as we forgive those who trespass against us," he did not halt or equivocate. Instead, he said, "Whoever did this, I forgive them." But, says Helen Prejean in recounting his story, "he acknowledges that it's a struggle to overcome the feelings of bitterness and revenge that well up, especially as he remembers David's birthday year by year and loses him all over again: David at 20, David at 25, David getting married; David standing at the back door with his little ones clustered around his knees, grown-up David, a man like himself, whom he will never know. He has learned that forgiveness is never going to be easy. Each day it must be prayed for and struggled for and won."[34]

For Further Reflection and Conversation

1. Where do you find the themes of liberation, connectedness, suffering, imagination, and repair of the world occurring in the Jubilee traditions of forgiveness?

2. Jubilee forgiveness is social and political as well as interpersonal. What does this add to our practices of forgiveness?

3. Why is it generally true that we cannot forgive ourselves? In what circumstances does that not hold true?

4. How do you respond to the idea that forgiveness is not always possible? Can you think of some examples of this?

5. What rituals of forgiveness have you discovered in the practice of your family life?

6. What rituals of forgiveness do you believe are necessary in community and religious life?

7. What rituals of forgiveness are necessary in national and international life?

4

Proclaim Liberty Throughout the Land to All Its Inhabitants

Prelude

Five traditions form the core of Jubilee teaching: fallow land, forgiveness, freedom, justice, and jubilation. In this book, I am proposing these traditions as the essential work of biblical people and as a religious vocation to which such people are called. It is not possible to pick and choose among the traditions, practicing one and neglecting another. Rather, as we examine each in turn, it becomes clear that these traditions coinhere; each is in all of the others. Forgiveness is an essential component in resting the land and in liberation; freedom comes with the remission of debt; letting the land lie fallow is a work of justice; and both justice and jubilation reside within the other four. Touch one Jubilee tradition and all the others quiver.

Furthermore, each of these traditions resounds through the sacred scriptures that have fashioned the religious lives of millions of people. This becomes clear if we place Jubilee in the center of the biblical tradition, and one way to understand Jubilee is as a gem or a jewel surrounded by crucial texts. Primary among these texts are the Sabbath laws, especially Ex. 20:8–11 and Deut. 5:12–15. As we saw in chapter 2, Jubilee demands the periodic rest of Sabbath if it is to occur at all, and Sabbath itself is so important that to the Jews, desecrating it equals desecrating all of Judaism.[1]

Other texts that resonate with Jubilee are those recognizing God as a liberator and celebrating the belief that Yahweh "saves." In Exodus this liberating God is confessed through freeing the Hebrew slaves and resting the land. As they do these things, the people of

Israel begin to figure out the moral and ethical implications of belonging to *this* God (Ex. 21:2–6; 23:10–11). As we saw earlier, Exodus 23 is not only about rest; it also prescribes an ethic of justice, since those who don't own land can harvest what grows spontaneously during the seventh year.

Other resonances of Jubilee occur in historical records documenting royal decrees of amnesty and release by neo-Assyrian and Akkadian kings who lived in the same regions as the early Hebrews and influenced their practices. According to these documents, release meant freedom from extreme indebtedness—the *deror* translated as "liberation." Another remarkable resonance is what Ringe refers to as the "prophetic amplification" of Jubilee found in Isaiah 58 and 61, where particular Jubilee injunctions are stressed.[2] Isaiah 58:6 reads, "Is not this the fast that I choose: to loose the bonds of injustice, to undo the thongs of the yoke, to let the oppressed go free"; and 61:1 reads, "He has sent me . . . to proclaim liberty to the captives, and release to the prisoners." All are promises repeated by Jesus and recorded not only in Luke 4:16–20 but throughout the Gospels.

In this larger setting of texts, a primary Jubilee tradition—perhaps the dominant Jubilee tradition—emerges. Just as it can be argued that the dominant motif of our closing century is liberation—political, economic, and religious—so it can be argued that the dominant motif of the biblical Jubilee is liberation—freedom, release, *deror*. No text heralds this Jubilee tradition more clearly than the one found in Leviticus 25 itself:

> You shall have the trumpet sounded throughout all your land. And you shall hallow the fiftieth year and you shall proclaim liberty throughout the land to all its inhabitants. It shall be a jubilee for you: you shall return, every one of you, to your property and every one of you to your family. . . . For it is a jubilee; it shall be holy to you.
>
> (Lev. 25:9b–10, 12a)

This primary Jubilee theme is the one we turn to now, the one inscribed on the Liberty Bell at Independence Hall in Philadelphia, Pennsylvania: "Proclaim liberty throughout the land to all its inhabitants."

This chapter is in two sections. The first pursues the question "For what does Jubilee free us?" Drawing on the text itself, it becomes clear that with the Jubilee we are free to go home, we are free to remember, and we are free for the re-creation in community that proceeds from Sabbath. The second directs attention to the two groups whose freedom is most often cited as the work of Jubilee liberation. A Jubilee people in a Jubilee world must give priority to freeing prisoners and to freeing children.

For What Does Jubilee Free Us?

Jubilee Frees Us to Go Home

The freedom to go home is mentioned three times in Leviticus 25. Verse 10b reads, "It shall be a jubilee for you: you shall return, every one of you, to your property and every one of you to your family." Verse 13 reads, "In this year of jubilee you shall return, every one of you, to your property." And verses 39–41, referring to people paying off their debts through their labor, say, "They shall serve with you until the year of the jubilee. Then they and their children with them shall be free from your authority; they shall go back to their own family and return to their ancestral property." In what follows, I focus on the meaning of this command for living the Jubilee today.

Few images in the human story are as moving as the exile returning home, whether it is Charles de Gaulle returning to Paris or Pablo Casals to Spain or Vladimir Horowitz to Moscow or Nelson Mandela to Johannesburg or Jean-Bertrand Aristide to Haiti. Home is a political image.

It is also a biblical image. It appears in the story of Naomi going back to Bethlehem and traveling with Ruth, who chooses a new home; it appears as well in the story of Naomi's other daughter-in-law, Orpah, who chooses to return to "her mother's home." (An interesting and unusual biblical note; Ruth 1:8.) It is in the story of the chastened Israelites returning from Babylon, who had once sat and wept on its shores remembering Zion. And it is in the account of Jesus returning to Nazareth, where he was brought up, and choosing to proclaim the Jubilee in his home synagogue.

But home is also an extraordinarily personal image, full of power and feeling. Surprisingly, and despite this, home is often a forgotten image in spirituality and in religious education. More often we are offered the journey, the quest, the going forth or the going out as guiding metaphors. These are, more typically, masculinized images that need to be complemented by images that arise from women's experience.

One theologian who has attended to the religious power of home is Kathryn Allen Rabuzzi. She points out that the business of housewifery is generally celebrated for its purposeful and productive side. But, she says, when we look at "home" work as having merit of its own, instead of as a kind of production, we notice the presence of ritual. And rituals are actions performed with regular rhythms. A woman or a man engaging regularly in the rhythmic patterns of homemaking finds that she or he shapes the rhythm of those actions and is, in turn, shaped by them, an outcome common to most rituals.[3]

Home is also the place we learn care and the "thicker times" of presence that care and Sabbath teach. "Thicker times," Rabuzzi says, "are what consistently fill the caretaker's life with dread. A back turned for just an instant can occasion irreversible damage, even death. The back door of a fourth-floor apartment momentarily left unlatched and a toddling two-year-old wanders out onto the unscreened fire escape; the spaghetti pot of boiling water left unwatched for just the moment it takes to walk across the floor to the phone; the Drano accidentally set under the bathroom sink instead of in the locked cabinet."[4]

Home is also the place where loneliness can be relieved through community, which is one profound meaning of the too often derided coffee klatch. It is also the place where homelessness can be understood in its truly heartbreaking dimension—by considering exactly what the *absence* of home means. Home is generally the place for lovemaking and, even more, for people-making, a task that often takes eighteen years, and usually, much longer. And for those who search beneath its many layers of meaning, the truest meaning of "coming home" is not a coming home to a mother or child, a lover or spouse; it is a coming home to oneself.

With reference to coming home to others, however, the Jubilee freedom to go home means going home to our people in at least two senses. First, it is a going home to our traditions, our ancestors, the people who have made us, *us*, even as it did for the first jubilarians. G. K. Chesterton wrote that "tradition may be defined as an extension of the franchise. Tradition means giving votes to the most obscure of all classes, our ancestors. It is the democracy of the dead. Tradition refuses to submit to the small and arrogant oligarchy of those who merely happen to be walking about."[5] Coming home to our tradition anchors us in history; for despite the adult ability to "see through" the flaws, mistakes, even the stupidity of our forebears, a tradition we can go home to is also an opportunity to "see through" in another sense.[6] A tradition is a lens that enables us to perceive reality by drawing on the gifts our predecessors have entrusted to us.

The other sense in which Jubilee frees us to go home is by providing the occasion to return to our parents. One of the most significant elements in the growing men's movement is the attention it gives to adult men's relations with their fathers. In the taped interview between Robert Bly and Bill Moyers called "A Gathering of Men," for instance—a tape requested from the Public Broadcasting System more often than any of its other videos—the central consideration is the father–son relation and the work of going home to embrace it and, where it has been marred, to mend it. And in the film *Quiz Show,* no scenes are more poignant that those between the damaged young man Charles Van Doren and his poet-father, Mark.

A related, but in other ways distinct, going home is women's return to our mothers. Whenever I have considered this theme with over-fifty women who are shaping a spirituality for life's second half, I have been moved by the profound attention they give to it. Almost universally, they recognize it as a piece of lifework they must do. Researcher Martha Robbins, interviewing adult women on the death of their mothers, discovered that women tended to mourn the *lives* of their mothers more than their *deaths*—especially their mothers' unfulfilled dreams, unspoken hopes, and lost opportunities.[7] Other women find going home an opportunity to learn their mother's story, especially when they have been estranged from her. The freedom to go home—in imagination or through the actual return—provides the opportunity to complete mourning or to let go of rejection.

The point of these comments is that many adults have unfinished business with our parents. And whereas the early adult years are more often about leaving the home of one's parents in order to make one's own, Jubilee is about returning to it. Jubilee offers a chance to address unfinished family business and is not unrelated, I suspect, to personal work that follows on the forty-ninth and fiftieth years of our own lives.

Still, there are other meanings of being free to go home. These include the freedom to create a spirituality for *this* time, the dawning twenty-first century, and *this* place—whether our place is Hong Kong, Melbourne, or Cleveland—at the same time that we learn the meaning of coming home to planet Earth. For as we complete the twentieth century and begin facing the twenty-first, where we have been given the photograph of the earth as seen from the moon—no boundaries—we are left with still another issue of going home that will be with us in the century to come. The issue is this: While honoring our individual anchorage and trying to be present in this place and time, as Sabbath teaches, can we come to the end of nationalism and patriotism as we have know them? Can we move to a common experience where we are free enough and liberated enough to call planet Earth our home?

That was a question answered in extremis by Etty Hillesum more than a Jubilee-time ago. She was the young Jewish woman who lived in Amsterdam but died in Auschwitz in 1943, and who left us her diary. And there she wrote what she had learned about home in the last two years of her life: "We *are* at home. Under the sky. In every place on earth, if only we can carry everything within us. We must be our own country."[8] When we discover that, the freedom to be at home, wherever we are, is ours.

Jubilee Frees Us to Remember

Jubilee liberation also means that we are free to remember, especially to remember captivity and release from captivity. As with the freedom to go home, this freedom is cited three times in Leviticus 25, and it is also a central motif elsewhere, notably in the book of Exodus, which gives it the status of a signature command: "Remember. You must remember." In Leviticus 25, the three citations—close in wording to the Exodus command—are in verses 38, 42, and 55: "I am the LORD your God, who brought you out of the land of Egypt, to give you the land of Canaan, to be your God"; "For they [those who worked for you] are my servants, whom I brought out of the land of Egypt"; and "For to me the people of Israel are servants; they are my servants whom I brought out from the land of Egypt."

Memory and remembering mean bearing witness and telling stories. Possibly, like going home, this work takes on special importance as human beings gather up our accumulating periods of seven years and approach and then pass the forty-ninth and fiftieth years, where personal developmental tasks like the life review, the use of reminiscence, and the composition of memoirs begin to claim us.

This work of storying is not only a personal task. It is an even more critical work in forming and continuing to be a people. It applies to such diverse communities as families celebrating fifty years in a new country, businesses remembering long-ago shoestring beginnings, and nations recalling release from slavery. In religious institutions, it applies to religious orders, local congregations, dioceses, and national denominations—all of which have stories to tell. It is not unusual for me to work with groups who engage in such storying as they celebrate 50th and even 100th anniversaries. In fact, I once celebrated the 150th year of their diocese—a triple Jubilee—with the Catholic people of Boise, Idaho.

Such human communities stress story's importance in their own creative lore. The Seneca tribe preserves the exchange "I go to hear stories." / "What are they?" / "I can't describe them, but if you come with me, you will know."[9]

Similarly, the Irish hold the belief that "a good story fills the belly," and the Eskimo teach that "stories chop off half the winter." Such storytelling is not a private or privatized task, however. Instead, it is done for the sake of the generations who follow us, especially as we preserve some stories, challenge others, and reinterpret still others. In my teaching I often use a tape titled "The Challenge of Memory," where five Holocaust survivors speak eloquently and from deep reservoirs of memory about their experiences and those of their families during those terrible years. On the night we viewed it in class during my semester in Cleveland, one of the graduate students said softly as we sat there together in silence, "I understand what this is like."

Then Ken told us that the previous summer, with his father, he had visited his father's ninety-year-old uncle, Ken's great-uncle. With tears streaming down his face, the old man remembered his mother for the younger men—the woman who was grandmother and great-grandmother to them. She'd been born into slavery, their uncle said, and when she was five, sold for five dollars. A father of small children himself, Ken repeated that, nodding his head: "Five years old. Five dollars."

This kind of remembering is particularly pertinent to Jubilee, for it is the nature of Jubilee to push to ever deeper dimensions of memory. That means that when I say, "Jubilee frees us to remember," I refer to at least three different forms this remembering takes.

The first is *dangerous* memory, of the kind taught by political theologian Johannes Baptist Metz. Metz coined the term to refer to those archetypal memories that make demands on us:

> There are memories in which earlier experiences break through to the centre-point of our lives and reveal new and dangerous insights for the present. They illuminate for a few moments and with a harsh steady light the questionable nature of things we have apparently come to terms with, and show up the banality of our supposed "realism." They break through the canon of the prevailing structures of plausibility and have certain subversive features. Such memories are like dangerous and incalculable visitations from the past. They are memories that we have to take into account, memories, as it were, with a future content.[10]

Among the different kinds of dangerous memory, Metz singles out two that Jubilee also insists on recalling: memories of suffering and memories of freedom. When the liberation of Jubilee touches us, it is finally safe to name these memories. It becomes safe to commemorate the terror of the first and to celebrate the joy of the second. Such memories free us for encounters with our own Egypts and our own Canaans as persons and communities, even as they freed our ancestors to encounter theirs and, eventually, to hand them on—to tradition them—to us.

A second form of remembering is *liturgical* memory, bringing the past into the present through the ritual task of re-member-ing, or *anamnesis*. The Passover seder with its ritual questions is the progenitor of this remembering, which is a work not so much of going back to the past as it is of making the past present to a gathered community. The Christian Eucharist with its central moment of anamnesis does the same, as the Christ is made present at the center of a people who ritualize the Christic presence by entering symbolically into the realities of bread broken and cup poured out.

The third form of remembering is *poetic* remembering, but the poetry is of a particular kind: the poetry of witness. The memories Jubilee points to are those that must not be forgotten. Instead, they must be testified to out of the seedbed of dangerous memory and the nourishment of liturgical memory. Many examples of the poetry of memory have recently become accessible in a collection published in 1993, although the poetry included has been a century in the making. Filled with reminiscence of the sobering corrective of suffering, the collection is titled *Against For-getting: Twentieth-Century Poetry of Witness.*[11] Its editor, Carolyn Forché, has gathered the work of 144 significant poets who en-dured conditions of historical and social extremity during the twentieth century—exile, state censorship, political persecution, house arrest, torture, imprisonment, military occupation, warfare, and assassination. "Many poets did not survive," Forché com-ments, "but their works remain with us as a poetic witness to the dark times in which they [and we] lived."[12]

The range of settings encompassed is vast and forms a great litany of events that have scarred the closing century. These include the Armenian genocide, World War I, revolution and repression in the Soviet Union, the Spanish Civil War, World War II, the Holo-caust/Shoah, repression in Eastern and Central Europe, war and dictatorship in the Mediterranean, the Indo-Pakistani Wars, war in the Middle East, repression and revolution in Latin America, the U.S. civil rights struggle, war in Korea and Vietnam, repression in Africa and the struggle against apartheid in South Africa, and rev-olutions and the struggle for democracy in China.

One of the poets represented is Chicano and Native American Jimmy Santiago Baca, orphaned as a child, on the streets at age eleven, and arrested for drug possession and intent to sell at twenty. Baca spent four years in solitary confinement in a maximum-security prison in Arizona. While in solitary he taught himself to read and write, and he eventually received a Wallace Stevens Yale Poetry fel-lowship. Out of the experience of oppression, Baca brings together the themes of suffering, memory, and witness to which Jubilee lib-eration summons.

Oppression

Is a question of strength,
of unshed tears,
of being trampled under,

and always, always,
remembering you are human.

Look deep to find the grains
of hope and strength,
and sing, my brothers and sisters,

and sing. The sun will share
your birthdays with you behind bars,
the new spring grass

like fiery spears will count your years,
as you start into the next year;
endure my brothers, endure my sisters.[13]

Jubilee Frees Us for Recreation in Community

The commentary on Leviticus 25 in *The New Interpreter's Bible* describes this third freedom: "The liberty proclaimed by Jubilee includes liberty or release from the toil of cultivating the land, for the land is to lie fallow all year long and produce only what comes up on its own without any sowing, cultivating, fertilizing or harvesting."[14] Put another way, we are free to keep the Sabbath (at least once in every fifty years a yearlong Sabbath, although two years may be better), and Sabbath is not only doing no-thing, not only rest and cessation from work. As we saw in chapter 2, Sabbath also includes *recreation in community*. This is the freedom where Jubilee challenges the artistic imagination to the vocation of repairing the world.

Rabbi Marc Gellman offers a midrash (a story about a story in the Bible) on creation that he calls "Partners" as a way of exploring what recreation means.[15] The midrash begins with the angels asking God to clean up the chaos that preceded creation, and after each major creative work—stars, oceans, four-legged animals—the angels ask God whether the world is finished yet. Regularly, God answers, "Nope." Eventually, God makes a woman and a man and says to them, "Please finish up the world for me. I'm tired now and really, it's almost done."

The man and woman at first resist this request, saying to God, "We can't do that. You have the plans and we are too little." So God agrees to a deal where if they keep trying to finish the world, God will be their partner. This divine–human partnership is described in the midrash as "finishing the world," but it is actually the work of repair and recreation to which the ending century challenges and for which Jubilee frees God's people. Sabbath is in the center of this freedom, meaning as it does that having contemplated the Creator of the world, we take up the vocation of recreating, repairing, and finishing it once the Sabbath is over.

The imagery of a Creator God who interacts with human beings and hands over to them a vocation as the world's "finishers" is familiar to poets and mystics. But the imagery does not assume this God withdrew from the created universe once it was done and washed the divine hands of it. Instead, the imagery assumes that the Creator is a brooding, hovering, indwelling presence in the midst of all human activity: renewing it, cherishing it, loving it. When we recognize our freedom to recreate God's world, we ought not think of ourselves as separated from the source of life. Rather, in recreating, we live and breathe and receive our own being with and in the Holy One. We "exercise" the divine presence, which, in the words of Julian of Norwich, and despite our extraordinary freedom, "is a love that clothes us, enfolds and embraces us, and . . . completely surrounds us, never to leave us."[16]

Thomas Berry, arguably the dean of this country's religious environmentalists, offers an important thesis on recreating in terms of contemporary theology. Speaking of theologies that have shaped our time, he notes that Western Europe gave the world the theology of redemption and Latin America gave the world the theology of liberation. But given its capacities for science, technology, communication, and invention, as well as its affinity for creation theology, it now looks as if North America may be destined to give the world a theology of creation.[17]

Such a theology would demand—and Berry's own work embodies this—that we create new relations to soil and water and air and all living things, relations that liberate them too. It would apply also to North Americans joining, for example, the northern Indian women who hug the trees to save them; the Kenyans who are part of the Green Belt movement to plant new trees, while the "developed nations" send bulldozers to tear them up; and the Fuji Grannies of Japan, who camp out trying to stop industrial building around Mount Fuji—they are the ancients who, when arrested, say, "We're not trying to make any trouble. We're too old."

But a theology of creation and recreation would also demand that we listen carefully to the entire liberation tradition of Jubilee. Not only does it say, "Proclaim liberty throughout the land"; it says, "Proclaim liberty throughout the land *to all its inhabitants*." And that cannot be done without recreating systems, structures, institutions, and practices that oppress or keep people from freedom. In this realization, recreation, like remembering, becomes dangerous; for it is not popular work to attempt to change the world, especially when this includes attempts to redress inequities among human beings. We have already seen this in the experience of Archbishop Oscar Romero. Or as another archbishop, Dom Helder Camera, the now retired pastoral leader from Recife, Brazil, is fond of saying, "When I feed the hungry I am called a saint. When I teach the hungry to read and to vote and to question their circumstances of poverty, I am a trouble-maker and a Communist."[18]

Nevertheless, Jubilee insists we are freed in order to proclaim liberty throughout the land to *all* its inhabitants, which includes questioning the structural and personal evil that fetters many and leaves others in various forms of bondage. Among these inhabitants, Jubilee singles out two groups: (1) prisoners—those who are captives, indentured servants, or enslaved Hebrews; and (2) children. They too are to be granted a liberty that allows them to go home, to remember, and to recreate their lives.

Those Whose Freedom Is a Priority

Proclaiming the Freedom of Prisoners

When we cross over into the land of Jubilee and respond to the vocation to become Jubilee people working for a Jubilee world, we are asked to work for the release of today's prisoners, indentured servants bound by law or contract, and undocumented aliens. Practicing hospitality, we are to give special care to strangers, too, who may feel like prisoners in a foreign land.

Tragically, this is the most flawed portion of the biblical Jubilee tradition, and whenever I meditate on Leviticus 25 I am struck by a rending and a tearing in the Jubilee fabric; for verses 44 through 46 carry the instruction:

> As for the male and female slaves whom you may have, it is from the nations around you that you may acquire male and female slaves. You may also acquire them from among the aliens residing with you, and from their families that are with you, who have been born in your land; and they may be your property. You may keep them as a possession for your children after you, for them to inherit as property. These you may treat as slaves, but as for your fellow Israelites, no one shall rule over the other with harshness.
>
> (Lev. 25:44–46)

Contemporary theology has taught us to name this blind spot as wrong and as sin: the teaching and practice of Jubilee today *does* assume the freeing of all enslaved persons. This is an example of how the Bible corrects itself out of its own principles. Still, we may be tempted to stand back from these verses horrified—or righteous— and ask, "How could they have been so oblivious? How could they have failed to recognize that these were enslaved *people*, even more as human beings, these were sisters and brothers? How could they have believed you could *own* other persons?"

Tempting, until we turn the questions of freedom and release back on ourselves and ask: What do we gloss over today? What are our sins of omission? What do we fail to see? Have we learned to pray regularly, "Free us, O God, from the narrowness of our vision. Help us to know what we see, not merely to see what we know"?

We can start this assessment many places, but an understanding of Jubilee provokes us to start with our prison systems and, for those of us who are U.S. Americans, to look at our soaring numbers of incarcerated persons where, as Elaine Roulet notes, "a rich boy's prank is a poor boy's felony." It provokes us to become aware that dehumanizing prison life takes the worst toll on the poorest in our midst and on their families—80 percent of the women in prison are mothers. This forges a connection between freeing prisoners and freeing children, who are what Roulet calls "the hidden victims of the penal system."[19]

If it is true that a nation's prisons reveal hidden, shadow sides of that nation while personal attitudes toward prisoners reveal hidden sides of our individual selves, it is necessary to ask why 76 percent of the U.S. population wants the death penalty, even though all other developed nations—most recently, South Africa—have abolished it. And if deterrence, rehabilitation, and retribution are the three reasons for imprisonment in the first place, why is retribution the one that appears to guide this country? Have we never reflected on the belief of Protagoras that the only reason for punishment is to teach people?

I have already cited Helen Prejean's eloquent book *Dead Man Walking*. One of the many reasons the book is so remarkable is that once you read it, you never forget the humanity of the imprisoned. You do not cease to be horrified, appalled, and repelled by particular crimes, but Prejean makes you see the offender's humanity. Another work, this one focusing on the false and unjust imprisonment of a simple man, is *A Lesson before Dying.*[20] The story is not only about the boy/man arrested at the scene of a murder he did not commit and eventually executed for it; it is also the tale of the small, poor community that loves and supports him through his agony and dying.

Both of these books impel toward action, and the good news is that there are people in our midst who have found ways to respond to this Jubilee command very specifically, people who are beacons of Jubilee. With scores of other women, many of whom are Catholic nuns, Elaine Roulet has bought and refurbished ten houses in and around Brooklyn, New York. Eight of these are called Providence House, where the residents are women who are ex-offenders, reunited with their children after the women have completed their sentences and taught job skills in preparation for productive work. The other two houses are called My Mother's House. Many of the children of still imprisoned women live in these, cared for by the resident adults, some of them sisters who are designated as foster parents. The name of these two houses makes it possible for a child whose mother is imprisoned to answer the question "Where do you live?" with the simple reply "I live at my mother's house."

Jean Harris is another beacon. In prison for thirteen years, she taught parenting classes and helped create a nursery and children's playroom while serving her sentence.[21] Now released, she runs a foundation for women prisoners and their children. And Dr. George Webber is the founder of a theological curriculum at Sing Sing prison that in the last twelve years has granted degrees in ministry to 145 men. The program is one of teaching and rehabilitation that prepares the students for jobs as chaplain's assistants, counselors, and teachers while in prison and for social-service jobs when they are released.

Gretchen Wolff Pritchard, minister of Christian nurture at St. Paul's Episcopal Church in New Haven, Connecticut, has written and published a children's illustrated lectionary for over ten years. Last Advent, when the Isaiah 61 text was the week's reading, she included in her lectionary an image of a barred door flung open and a ragged and emaciated figure leaping through it into the sunlight, with uplifted hands and a joyous face. When the picture appeared, she received a letter from a parent that read, in part:

> I don't feel the average kid reading this will come away with the idea of "set at liberty those who are oppressed." My eight-year-old son's interpretation was more like "open up

the jails and let everybody go." I'm not so sure Charles
Manson and Ted Bundy fall into the oppressed category.[22]

Commenting on that parent's letter, Pritchard said the father didn't
make it clear whether the child thought opening up the prisons and
freeing everyone was bad news or good. But she did point out that
the nightmare of murderers let loose (whether that was the parent's or the child's nightmare wasn't clear) was based on historical
misunderstanding, for in the Bible, prisoners are not criminals or
convicts, because incarceration was not the penalty for civilian
criminal acts. Rather, they were prisoners of war or of conscience,
debtors, captives, hostages, victims of militarism or government
oppression. Pritchard concluded by suggesting that children,
more attuned to the imaginative world than many adults, tend to
grasp this intuitively and identify prisoners "as innocent good
guys unjustly held, awaiting rescue by friends who are saying,
'We've got to save them!'"[23]

But not all prisoners today are innocent good guys—they have
done terrible things. Still, the command stands: Proclaim liberty
throughout the land to all its inhabitants; free the prisoners from
bondage. We who are Jews and Christians and have a long line of
convicted felons in our religious ancestry need to find ways—like
some of those described here—to help those prisoners return
home, to themselves and to forgiveness and to interior freedom; to
come to terms with their memories; and to re-create their lives. At
the same time, we need to read this tradition as counseling us to
turn inward and examine our own chains, our own bondage, and
the cells we build in our souls.

Proclaiming the Freedom of Children

The Jubilee tradition of liberating children is built into the text
through the words "they *and their children with them* shall be free"
(v. 41) or "shall go free" (v. 54), found in Leviticus 25. The situation of children in our world has tragic parallels to that of the children whom the original Jubilee provision sought to liberate. Four
thousand years later, children continue to be exploited in obscene
and inhuman ways, making this command especially urgent today.

Karen Love, a professor at Western Wyoming College, reports a
conversation she overheard while on a recent flight from Cuba to
Mexico. "'Six is way too young,' said the American businessman,

laughing," she reports. "Twelve is the youngest I'd take . . . maybe 11, but 6 is too young." He was talking about prostitutes in Cuba, where many people have only enough rationed food to last half the month. In their hopelessness, families sometimes send their children to the streets to sell their bodies—their poverty not unrelated to the U.S. government's treatment of that island nation. What about those children?[24]

Anna Quindlen, a Pulitzer Prize–winning former *New York Times* columnist, raises the issue this way: "Would you buy a rug if you knew that it had been woven in India by 10-year-olds beaten if they didn't work fast enough? Would you wear a shirt if it had been sewn by a 9-year-old locked into a factory in Bangladesh until production quotas for the day had been met? Would you eat sardines if the cans had been filled by 12-year-old Filipino children sold into bonded servitude?"[25]—the servitude Jubilee sought to abolish. The questions arise from consideration of GATT (the General Agreement on Tariffs and Trade), the free-trade pact, and the largely unsuccessful move to attach "Not manufactured with child labor" on all products coming under the treaty. What about those children?

In California, voters have passed Proposition 187, refusing schooling and medical care to the children of illegal immigrants (the proposition's desired outcome has been stayed by the courts as of this writing). What about those children?

Each of these situations cries for redress: each is bad, intolerable news. Yet similar to cases cited concerning prisoners, there is good news here too. It is the news of those who hear and respond to the cries of the children.

I have many personal heroes among these respondents. One is Molly Rush, who introduced me to the question that is best shouted here, rather than raised quietly: *What about the children?* Rush, the mother of six and grandmother of two, was director of the Thomas Merton Peace Center in Pittsburgh, Pennsylvania, for some years and because of that role often was asked to join community efforts and demonstrations protesting the proliferation of nuclear arms, warheads, missiles, and submarines—the whole demonic array of lethal weapons our society has created. Her response was always the same. She would think of her family of six and say, "I'm sorry; I can't go with you—what about the children?" One day she heard her own question with reference not to the time given for the protest but to the impact of the weapons on her own children and the children of the world. And so she began to raise this question publicly.[26]

Another hero is Jean Donovan, one of four churchwomen killed in El Salvador in 1980, who wrote the month before her death, "The Peace Corps left today and my heart sank low. The danger is extreme and they were right to leave. . . . Now I must assess my own position, because I am not up for suicide. Several times I have decided to leave. I almost could, except for the children, the poor bruised victims of adult lunacy. Who would care for them? Whose heart would be so staunch as to favor the reasonable thing in a sea of their tears and helplessness? Not mine, dear friend, not mine."[27]

I meet heroes like Rush and Donovan regularly—I suspect we all do. At the end of one Tuohy lecture, for example, an old friend stopped on her way out to tell me about her daughter. Just graduated from the University of Notre Dame, the young woman was spending all of the next year working at a shelter for abused women and their children, before going on to law school the following year. Another evening, discussing how we might be Jubilee people, a woman told all of us of her work with survivors of child abuse.

Other times, the Jubilee work of liberating children comes from large organizations. One is UNICEF (United Nations Children's Fund), which has almost single-handedly eliminated death through dysentery for the world's children. Another is the Children's Defense Fund (CDF), whose work embodies each of the traditions of Jubilee but is particularly creative in working to liberate children from bondage. In 1991 the CDF held the first national observance of the Children's Sabbath. This observance, held every year since throughout this country, seeks to lift a united voice of concern for children by exploring the religiously based imperative to speak out on behalf of the vulnerable and to encourage a commitment to help children and families through prayer, education, service, and advocacy.

The Children's Sabbath observance begins with Shabbat services on a designated Friday each October and concludes with church services the following Sunday, during which congregations across the nation hold special services, education programs, and related activities on how people of faith can respond to children's needs. In 1994 the Sabbath theme was stopping the gun war against children, in the light of the urgent need in the United States to protect children from violence. The way this was—and is—done is through a wide range of options, from giving out very detailed lesson plans for children, adolescents, and adults (prepared specifically for Catholic, Protestant, Jewish, African American, and Latina congregations), to creating banners or other memorials with the names of all the children in the area who have been killed by violence over the past year, to ringing a bell or asking the local fire department to sound its siren every two hours on the Children's Sabbath in memory—dangerous memory—of the children who are killed by violence in the United States every two hours.[28]

Along with government protest against the sex trade and child labor, these are ways to proclaim liberty throughout the land to all its inhabitants, so that the youngest prisoners in our midst might be released from bondage. Then they, and in years to come, their children with them, may be able to return home, with their memories, their creativity, and their freedom intact.

For Further Reflection and Conversation

1. Where do you find the theme of liberation characteristic of this century in relation to the Jubilee teaching to proclaim liberty throughout the land to all its inhabitants?

2. Where do you find the themes of connectedness, suffering, imagination, and repair of the world reflected in this teaching?

3. When you exercise the freedom to go home, to what traditions do you find yourself returning? To which people? Why and how are they sources of liberation in your life?

4. How have you been educated to use the freedom to remember? Which of your memories do you consider dangerous ones? Where have rituals of memory educated you?

5. What freedoms to recreate draw your attention? What recreation do you believe is needed in the institutions you belong to, for example, your church, your neighborhood, your country?

6. How do you practice a spirituality that takes seriously the freedom of prisoners? In what ways, if any, is this linked to personal or private prisons or bondage in your life?

7. In what ways do you practice a spirituality that takes seriously the freedom of children?

5

Jubilee Justice

Prelude

In the three preceding chapters, I have used the same pattern, beginning each with a set of comments that refer to Jubilee as a whole. Only then do I move to the particular Jubilee tradition that is the focus of the chapter. Before considering the fallow land and the Sabbath, I wrote of Jubilee appearing throughout the world like a starburst, from the World Council of Churches considering it as its theme for 1998 to the Vatican planning repentance as essential to the "Grand Jubilee" of the year 2000. In considering forgiveness, I began with a primer of key Jubilee terms. And in reflecting on freedom, I set Jubilee in the midst of a number of related scripture passages that are treasures for those who would be Jubilee people today, seeking to create a Jubilee world.

In this chapter, as prelude to considering Jubilee justice, I continue this pattern. Here my preliminary comments concern Jubilee as both a curriculum of religious education and a form of spirituality. I speak briefly of each of these themes and stress the contemporary belief that justice is an essential component of both.

With reference to education, especially religious education, Jubilee includes what are—or ought to be—essential components of all religious education: contemplative quiet, or Sabbath; forgiveness; freedom; justice; and the jubilation and festivity that are commonly expressed in liturgy and worship. These teachings, or disciplines, can serve as a curriculum for classrooms and schools but are not limited to these settings. They also can serve the family as it educates, and they can serve parishes and congregations, businesses, and nations. Each of these settings provides a forum for educating *to* the Jubilee traditions and *through* the Jubilee traditions.

But Jubilee also comprises a spirituality. I use the term *spirituality* to refer to our way of being in the world in the light of the Mystery at the core of the universe; a mystery that some of us call God. The term also includes understanding what that Mystery requires of us, such as the classic set of demands recorded in Micah 6:8: "to do justice, and to love kindness, and to walk humbly with your God."

As readers know, a phenomenal and renewed interest in spirituality has gripped the entire U.S. culture since the late 1960s, although the term *spirituality* as it is used in the society has at least two quite different meanings. One is characterized by withdrawal, turning inward, parochialism, and attending to God and one's inner self. Such a spirituality lacks a social and political dimension and is sometimes undergirded by a conviction that the world is too much with us and that "worldly" involvement is dangerous, even destructive.

The second contemporary meaning of spirituality is quite different. If anything, it assumes a way of being in the world that demands even deeper involvement and immersion in the world than is usual, drawing on the belief that everything that is, is holy— although not yet completely so. This second form of spirituality is "noisy"[1] and based on a conviction that those who withdraw their hands make them dirty. Many who practice it believe that this was the spirituality of the people from whom Jesus came, of Jesus himself, and of the followers of Jesus, who taught (the grounding for the belief is in Gen. 2:7) that God formed human beings from the dust of the earth and then breathed the divine breath into the dust. That is how we came into life.

Or as poet-farmer Wendell Berry has written, when God made us, God did not make us body and soul, with the soul slipped into the body like a letter slipped into an envelope. Instead, God made us from an inseparable mix of "dust and breath." Our holiness comes from keeping these two sources together: the divine breath coursing within us mingles with the prosaic but sacred dust we share with all the other earth creatures, dust that originated as particles of a massive star. Dust and breath make us "members of the holy community of creation," and the dustier and breathier we are, the better.[2]

In addition to this composite makeup that describes our persons, another factor shapes this form of spirituality: the conviction that spirituality necessarily includes works that serve justice. It is not justice imagined as a blindfolded figure trying to balance a set of scales arbitrarily, however. Instead, it is a fiery, prophetic, unrelenting justice, urged on us by a God of justice who demands not only that we preach it but that we do it. Justice is not only a constituent dimension of the gospel, it is a constituent dimension of religious education and spirituality. It is also a constituent dimension of Jubilee.

Having made these preliminary comments, I turn to the work of this chapter. First I offer a brief reflection on biblical understandings of justice and on one specific meaning that Jubilee emphasizes: in Walter Brueggemann's phrase, Jubilee justice requires us "to sort out what belongs to whom and to return it to them."[3] Then I explore some of the implications Jubilee justice has religiously, economically, and socially. I conclude with a coda on mourning as a necessary moment in the lives of those who would live out a jubilarian commitment to a just, Jubilee world.

Biblical Understandings of Justice

Singling out justice as a particular theme in the Bible has a wry, even paradoxical side to it. I once taught with a biblical scholar in Oregon, and one night a student asked him to name the most important texts on justice from the Hebrew Bible. His response has remained with me since: "It's very difficult to do that," he answered. "The entire Bible is about justice."

Nevertheless, we can examine some of the influences that inform biblical justice. The first of these is prophecy. The prophets never preach a watered-down justice and only rarely a gentle justice: for them, justice is passionate, tempestuous, hotheaded, and, most of all, immediately necessary. Prophecy is a particular kind of work, with that work situated physically on the lips and the mouth, symbolizing a demand for utterance. In Isa. 6:6 the prophet recalls his anointing to it: "Then one of the seraphs flew to me, holding a live coal that had been taken from the altar with a pair of tongs. The seraph touched my mouth with it and said: 'Now that this has touched your lips, your guilt has departed and your sin is blotted out.'"

Isaiah's anointing symbolizes his recognition that prophecy is about speaking and living the word, especially speaking the word *no* to all that destroys and living the prophetic *no* with all one's might, refusing to let false words and false actions slip by without comment and resistance.

In my judgment, no one describes prophecy more eloquently than Rabbi Abraham Joshua Heschel (ironically, the same thing can be said for his description of Sabbath: Jewish mysticism and Jewish morality are as inseparable as dust and breath). Heschel says that prophecy is born from the *pathos* of God.[4] This divine pathos or grief—too much for both God and the prophet to ignore—contributes to making prophetic teaching bothersome and troublesome; for prophecy causes both temple authorities and ordinary people to feel uncomfortable. As Heschel describes the situation, they read the Bible for a sense of order, but instead of getting it, they are thrown into

> orations about widows and orphans, about the corruption of judges and affairs of the market place. Instead of showing us a way through the elegant mansions of the mind, the prophets take us to the slums. The world is a proud place, full of beauty, but the prophets are scandalized, and rave as if the whole world were a slum. They make much ado about things, lavishing excessive language upon trifling subjects.[5]

Then Heschel makes his point: "The things that horrify the prophets are even now daily occurrences all over the world."[6]

Prophets make temple authorities and ordinary people uncomfortable. One of the most dramatic examples of this occurs in the primary New Testament Jubilee text, the fourth chapter of Luke's Gospel. Verses 16–20 are familiar to most people. But if we read past them, we come across an account of grumbling and murmuring on the part of the congregants. And as Jesus develops his reflection on the text of Isaiah in relation to what it means for that ordinary congregation, they start to mutter the Aramaic equivalent of "Who does he think he is?" They move to expel him, the movement catches fire, and they attempt to throw him out bodily, not only from the synagogue but from Nazareth and even from life. And why? Because he was calling them to justice.

In the Bible many words are associated with justice. The Hebrew word for justice is *mispat,* which has a variety of meanings such as "justice," "judgment," "rights," "vindication," "deliverance," and "custom." Strong evidence exists, however, that originally *mispat* referred to the restoration of a situation or an environment that promoted equity and harmony—shalom—in a community. It is a word regularly found in the Psalms and in the words of the prophets, especially when God is portrayed as having a special concern for the poor, the widow, the fatherless, and the oppressed. It refers to basic human rights and to the restorative acts of repairing the world.[7]

However, *mispat* is not the only word used in the Bible to help us understand justice, and the justice of Yahweh is not in contrast to other covenant qualities such as steadfast love (*hesed*), mercy (*rahamin*), or faithfulness (*emunah*).[8] In many texts it is virtually equated with them. Indeed, when they try to elaborate on the meaning of justice, many theologians are almost rhapsodic in their expressions. Gerhard von Rad, for example, writes, "There is absolutely no concept in the Old Testament with so central a significance for all relationships of human life as that of *sedaqah* [justice/righteousness]."[9] And John Donahue points out that terms for justice are applied to a wide variety of things. Scales or weights are called just when they give a fair measure, and paths are called just when they do what a path or way should do—lead to a destination. Laws are just not because they conform to an external norm or constitution but because they create harmony within the community. And human beings are just when we practice fidelity to the demands of a relationship.[10]

In speaking of justice as fidelity to the demands of a relationship, Donahue writes:

> In contrast to modern individualism the Israelite is in a world where "to live" is to be united with others in a social context either by bonds of family or by covenant relationships. This web of relationships—king with people, judge with complainants, family with tribe and kinfolk, the community with the resident alien and suffering in their midst, and all with the covenant God—constitutes the world in which life is played out.[11]

But it is Walter Brueggemann's terse phrase that provides the clearest and closest rendering of Jubilee justice: you find out what belongs to whom and give it back. Brueggemann fleshes out this meaning by telling a prosaic story of a very proper woman who went to a tea shop one day, sat down, ordered tea, and got ready to eat some cookies that she carried in her purse.

> Because the tea shop was crowded, a man took the other chair and also ordered tea. As it happened, he was a Jamaican black, though that is not essential to the story. The woman was prepared for a leisurely time, so she began to read her paper. As she did so, she took a cookie from the package. As she read, she noticed that the man across also took a cookie from the package. This upset her greatly, but she ignored it and kept reading. After a while she took another cookie. And so did he. This unnerved her and she glared at the man. While she glared, he reached for the fifth and last cookie, smiled and offered her half of it. She was indignant. She paid her money and left in a great hurry, enraged at such a presumptuous man. She hurried to her bus stop just outside. She opened her purse to get her fare. And then she saw, much to her distress, that in her purse was her package of cookies unopened.[12]

Brueggemann concludes the story by making the point that we are not very different from that woman. Sometimes we possess things so long that we come to think of them as ours, even though they don't belong to us. But at other times, "by the mercy of God, we have occasion to see to whom these things in fact belong. And when we see that, we have some little chance of being rescued from our misreading of reality."[13]

For those of us who are so privileged we have forgotten who owns what, Jubilee justice comes as a gift; for the particular meaning of justice that Jubilee stresses is the notion of "return," not in the Jubilee journey sense of a return home but return as relinquishing, giving back, and handing over what is not ours to God and to those crying for justice throughout the whole, round earth.

Implications of Jubilee Justice

The Jubilee text of Leviticus 25 offers several descriptions that elaborate on what finding out and giving back entail:

> When you buy from your neighbor, you shall pay only for the number of years since the jubilee; the seller shall charge

you only for the remaining crop years. If the years are
more, you shall increase the price, and if the years are
fewer, you shall diminish the price; for it is a certain number of harvests that are being sold to you.

(vv. 15–16)

The land shall not be sold in perpetuity, for the land is
mine; with me you are but aliens and tenants.

(v. 23)

Throughout the land that you hold, you shall provide for
the redemption of the land.

(v. 24)

If anyone of your kin falls into difficulty and sells a piece
of property, then the next of kin shall come and redeem
what the relative has sold. If the person has no one to redeem it, but then prospers and finds sufficient means to do
so, the years since its sale shall be computed and the dif-
ference shall be refunded to the person to whom it was
sold, and the property shall be returned.

(Lev. 25:25–27)

Clearly, these texts make two striking points. One is their provision of an answer to the question "How long does my ownership
last?" where the reply is "No more than fifty years." Because everything in the universe is gift, you're allowed to buy only a certain
number of harvests, for—as Yahweh succinctly puts it—"the land
is mine." The other point, however, is that at the time the Jubilee
was first proclaimed, what the modern world refers to as "capital"
was equivalent to land. Land that originally belonged to others
must be returned to them.

Most commentators agree this rendering of Jubilee's meaning—
the restoration of land—can't always be applied exactly today, although obviously there are occasions when land can and should be
returned. But to see this as the only expression of Jubilee justice
would entail limiting the modern meaning of capital or possessions
to land; perhaps even more difficult—indeed, impossible—it
would also assume a continuously equal population throughout
the world, with the same number of people alive from one century
to the next.

Commentators are also agreed that we can make contemporary
applications of Jubilee justice, seeking to embody its moral princi-

ples today—the fact that the scripture cannot always be taken literally does not sanction washing our hands of the vocation to justice. More specifically, we can apply the precepts of Jubilee justice religiously, economically, and socially. I will comment briefly on the first area, then expand on how we might do justice by finding out what belongs to whom economically and socially.

Justice and the Religious Realm

This entire book is a reflection on the religious meaning of Jubilee, and implicitly, on Jubilee justice. Here I simply add that the knowledge of ourselves as forgiven by God, a knowledge fostered by keeping the Sabbath, is expected to issue in practical forgiveness of debts, even as the Hebrews were expected to release others from similar bondage. The religious character of this is underscored by the fact the Jubilee was proclaimed on the Day of Atonement, even as religious communities today are starting to choose significant times when they will proclaim Jubilee, notably the new millennium. Understanding Jubilee religiously—then and now—requires that people dwell in God's creative presence; trust God's liberating action while recognizing it usually occurs through human beings; experience God's forgiveness; hope in God's promises; and practice God's justice. Religious wholeness characterizes Jubilee.[14]

Justice and the Economic Realm

The commentary on Jubilee's implication for religious justice in the Anchor Bible series also speaks to what God required of Israel economically. It describes "what in principle God desires for humanity—broadly equitable distribution of the resources of the earth, especially land, and a curb on the tendency to accumulate, with its inevitable oppression and alienation. The Jubilee stands as a critique not only of massive private accumulation of land and related wealth, but also of large-scale forms of collectivism or nationalization which destroy any meaningful sense of personal or family ownership."[15]

When we examine this statement, we see at least three faces of Jubilee justice, viewed economically. One face is the *oikumenē*, or the whole round earth—what today is the focus of *ecology*. The second face is *economy*, meaning the realm of human householding. The third face is *economics*, what today we call *the* economy.

The *Oikumenē*

The Greek word *oikumenē* comes from the noun *oikos*—a "house" or "dwelling"—and the verb *oikeo*—"to live" or "to dwell." Usually, the word is translated as "the whole inhabited world," but human arrogance has often led to forgetting that this inhabitation includes others besides ourselves. Bugs and buffalo, rivers and rocks, also inhabit the whole, round earth.

Thomas Berry writes that if we are dealing with economics as a religious issue, we can deal with it in different ways. One is to start with the capitalist market economy's neglect of its social responsibilities and to emphasize our social and political responsibilities to ensure that the weak and less gifted are not exploited by the strong and the competent. The other is to start with an even more basic difficulty underlying the social issues: the industrial economy itself, which in its present form is not a sustainable economy. Though we need to attend to budget deficits, Jubilee justice reminds us that underneath them lies the earth deficit. About this deficit Berry writes:

> Seldom does anyone speak of the deficit involved in the closing down of the basic life system of the planet through abuse of the air, the soil, the water, and the vegetation. [But] the earth deficit is the real deficit, the ultimate deficit, the deficit in some of its major consequences so absolute as to be beyond adjustment from any source in heaven or on earth. . . . This deficit in its extreme expression is not only a resource deficit, but the death of a living process, not simply the death of *a* living process but of *the* living process.[16]

Berry concludes that today, in contrast to previous generations, our problem vis-à-vis this deficit is definitively different, because we human beings are determining the destiny of the earth—with all its inhabitants—in an irreversible manner. "The immediate danger is not *possible* nuclear war," he writes, "but *actual* industrial plundering."[17]

Thus, in the first instance, "find out what belongs to whom and give it back" means return what belongs to the soil, the water, the air, and the earth, and to all of nonhuman nature.

Economy

As I use this term here, I refer not to the economy as wealth, capital, and resources but to the ways of human housekeeping and human householding—home—and to the ways the human household is situated and maintained within the household of nature. Here a Jubilee people must find out what workable answers exist to those who say we cannot live without the market economy that is destroying us and our world—issues already raised by ecology and our responsibility to the *oikumenē*.

Issues of economy as human householding are deeply tied to issues of the artistic imagination, especially as we use that imagination in the repair and recreation of the world. Wendell Berry describes this relation by referring to art as all the different ways human beings make the things they need: "How we work, what work we do, how well we use the materials we use, and what we do with them after we have used them—all these questions are of the gravest religious significance."[18]

Berry probes this significance by elaborating on the spirituality of dust and breath, saying that if we believe we are God's dust and God's breath, then each of our acts has a supreme significance; for "if it is true that we are living souls, then all of us are artists. All of us are makers, within mortal terms and limits, of our lives, of one another's lives, of things we need and use."[19] Those who work with words to preach a sermon, those who work with a team of horses to plow the land, those who set up an easel to paint a canvas—all have a cosmic function, because all are makers.

In this understanding of economy, work is critical—that work which is partner to Sabbath, the work of recreation in community. Finding out what belongs to whom and giving it back means finding out the holiness of our own work—whatever it is—and how we might give that to the community of creation through the religious vocation of repairing the world. But it also involves the discovery that not everyone is free to work. And that leads, eventually, to *the* economy, or economics.

Economics

"Economics" refers here to the most commonly assumed aspect of the economy, the arena of capital, wealth, land, and goods—including money but not limited to money. It also refers to the economically translatable value of the schooling, education, skills, health, opportunities, and privilege that bring these to some but not to all.

One of the privileges often accorded Nobel Prize–winning economists is the assumption they are the only ones who understand economics—an assumption that is not the fault of the economists. A recent *New York Times* account helped to question this with the following story, filed under the heading "Camp Lemonade Stand":

> The season is late summer. Billy and Sue decide to sell lemonade in front of the house. They measure out water and sugar. They make a sign all by themselves and prop it up on a crate.
>
> Or: They go to lemonade camp. . . . On the principle that successful entrepreners need early encouragement and training, Loyola College in Maryland created Camp Lemonade Stand. This summer, in two separate weeklong sessions, groups of 6-to-10-year-olds were taught researching, marketing, advertising, business strategies and a few recipes.
>
> "Kids this age are very entrepreneurial," says a dean of the college. So are colleges. The camp costs $250 per child, and children learn the differences between net and gross when they pay back $10 in seed money out of their proceeds.
>
> But it's all for a good cause. Underlying this capitalism is philanthropy. All the proceeds from Camp Lemonade Stand go to Project Mexico—two orphanages the college sponsors in Mexico.[20]

This is preparation for understanding and becoming involved in the economic life of one's own country and of other countries. Indeed, these youngsters may be at the beginning of understanding just how much the U.S. relations with Mexico is tied to the land that belonged to Mexico until the nineteenth century, when warfare, expansion, and sale made Mexican land part of the United States. It may be difficult to imagine a legal means of restoring such land today, but to be unaware of the Jubilee connection is to miss the creation of just possibilities.[21]

For the ordinary person, the beginnings of this creativity lie in guidelines being developed throughout today's world that assist people in determining how they might find out what belongs to whom and give it back. Among these guidelines are the following:

1. There are limits to growth. Environmentally concerned scientists throughout our world have given widespread publicity to

this principle via the "limits to growth" theory, concerning what is and is not sustainable life on this planet.[22] But further education is undoubtedly needed concerning the metaphor of growth itself. On the one hand is the image of growth embodied in all living creatures, both human and nonhuman: we are born; we grow to a certain height, weight, and fruitfulness; we decline; we die. Such is the organic, healthy meaning of the metaphor. On the other hand we have a cancer metaphor of growth: growth as the unlimited proliferation of diseased cells. Although disease-as-metaphor has its own problems, the imagery of the unhealthy proliferation of cancer cells helps develop understanding of the dangers of unlimited growth in the same ways as do unstoppable giantism or obesity.

2. There are limits to earning. A recent conversation with friends led to two different proposals on this issue. Catherine said that everyone in the nation, including those working at home giving care to children, ought to get the same salary. Dick proposed that the highest salaries should go to those doing the most menial and least desired labor, whereas those whose work is most intrinsically satisfying should receive the least. But both believed in a salary cap.

   Herman Daly, an economist with years of service at the World Bank, talks as many others do of ratios in earning, what is sometimes called "limited inequality." Daly points out that the military and civil service in this country both earn at a ratio of around ten to one: the highest paid member of the military makes no more than ten times the lowest paid member. In academic circles the ratio is around seven to one, with distinguished professors earning no more than seven times the salary of the lecturers who have not yet finished their dissertations (unless the lecturer is an adjunct professor, often the serf of academia, who is generally grossly underpaid by the feudal university).[23] These ratios are in sharp contrast to CEOs' salaries—the chair of General Motors versus the assembly-line auto worker—or to entertainers' salaries—David Letterman and Oprah Winfrey both earn more than ten times the bit player in a TV soap. Salary imbalances became a national issue during the baseball strike of the mid-1990s, not only when it became clear that the star with the contract for $7 million a

year earned many times more than the large number of players
making $120,000 but when it became impossible to find out
the salaries that owners paid to themselves.

3. There are limits to accumulation. As we have seen, the Jubilee
   is pertinent and practical here, answering the question "How
   much can I acquire?" with the response "Only what you can
   accumulate in fifty years." This means that a will can either be
   a Jubilee document or create further division of rich and poor,
   especially in the case of inherited but unearned wealth. But Jubilee can also guide businesses and corporations. In October
   1994, for example, a consortium of semiconductor companies
   volunteered to give up (return, relinquish, give back) a $90-
   million-a-year federal subsidy. The consortium, Sematech, was
   created seven years earlier to encourage U.S. production of
   semiconductors. As a result, it began to produce them, and by
   1994 the future of the industry was assured. So Sematech decided to stop the subsidy on the principle that they did not
   need it anymore.[24]

   This guideline is pertinent to the accumulation of land. As I
   have noted, it is sometimes possible to restore actual land even
   today: among the most dramatic examples in this century are the
   returns to the original inhabitants of former colonial nations in
   Africa, the British withdrawal from the subcontinent of India,
   and the U.S. relinquishment of the Philippines. This Jubilee tradition is about land redistribution whenever possible, whether
   to North American natives; to natives of countries richer nations
   have despoiled, including those whose economies they have
   devastated; or to countries taken as spoils of war.

   Sarah Epperly, a California writer, suggests other aspects of
   restoring land: "Society might begin to live in such a manner
   that the reverence for life of native tribes would reemerge. We
   might begin on a personal level by eating only the amount of
   food required to live a healthful life, so that we want not but
   also waste not. We might use laundry detergents that don't pol-
   lute streams. We might imitate white-water rafting practices
   that must leave the water and shoreline exactly as it was, even
   to carrying off ashes from the campfire."[25]

4. There are no limits to all people having the right to certain ben-
   efits: literacy; education in basic skills, including basic economics; a job; life, liberty, and the pursuit of happiness. One

of these rights is health care; it is difficult to understand how congressional lawmakers continue to evade this, since their own health care and that of their families is so extensive. Still another basic is the right to water. One of the first articles of agreement when Israel and Jordan signed the draft of their wide-ranging peace treaty in this decade was the simple headline "Will Share Water."

5. There are also—apparently—no limits to two other things. The first is human resistance when faced with the theology of relinquishment, where the demand on our lives is to simplify and to give back in order to redress massive inequality. But the other unlimited factor is the human imagination—especially the North American human imagination, with its can-do dimension—in finding out how to live this Jubilee tradition by sorting out what belongs to whom and returning it.

Some of the people I have met who talk about Jubilee in their lives provide simple yet eloquent examples here: the woman who told me that she and her husband had sold their second house because two homes in this needy world seemed an obscenity; the couple who have given up on stocks and bonds to invest in the schooling of a child in a family not their own, because that child is poor; the lawyers at our local soup kitchen, who make their pro bono services available to everyone who needs them; the Salvadoran peasants who receive all visitors as ambassadors from the Divine and give up the best spots on their earth floor to their guests while they sleep outside. All are aware that "the earth is the Lord's," and all have found ways to honor this and to give back whatever they can.

Justice and the Social Realm

This brief sketch of some of the economic implications of Jubilee justice already foreshadows many of its social implications. Still, one social unit must be stressed and highlighted, the same one stressed in the biblical teaching: the family. Essentially, Jubilee articulates a specific, practical concern for the family, one we have already encountered in considering forgiveness from debt.

Families' lives are badly damaged if they are split up by economic forces that make them powerless, making restoration of social dignity to families through economic viability still another aim of Jubilee justice. Further, the economic collapse of a family in one generation ought not be the circumstance, as it is in much of our world today, that condemns all future generations to perpetual debt.

Although economics can never be completely separated from family life, Jubilee justice does apply to families in other personal and intimate areas. For older family members, the principle of finding out/giving back turns attention to the generations coming after us. In Richard Ford's novel *Wildlife*, for example, a mother tries to teach this Jubilee tradition to her son. As her marriage is ending, she says to the sixteen-year-old, "Your life doesn't mean what you have, sweetheart, or what you get. It's what you're willing to give up. That's an old saying, I know. But it's still true." When he responds that he feels that's a problem for him, since he doesn't want to give up anything, she goes on, "Oh well. Good luck." Then she elaborates: "That's really not one of the choices," she says. "You have to give things up. That's the rule. It's the major rule for everything."[26]

One of my colleagues, a New Jersey educator, describes what this has meant in her family. She told me that finding out what belongs to whom and returning it became real for her when her oldest daughter came home after her first year in college. "The first weeks she was home," my colleague said, "I found myself encountering reluctance on her part to account for her time, especially how long she'd be gone in the evening and when she was coming in. I finally realized that accountability now belongs to her; that made it possible for me to give it back."

At the same time, adult children experience the relevance of finding out and giving back with reference to the generations preceding them, especially toward their parents. Often a bittersweet moment comes in adult life when we need to return to our parents their wishes for us, their dreams for us—of schooling, of a mate, of lifework, for example—so that we might pursue our own. Even more poignant and powerful, a finding-out moment also occurs with their deaths, as we return their bodies or their ashes to the earth.

This Jubilee teaching even reveals individual, intrapersonal dimensions that we may not have suspected or, more likely, have not had time to consider. Often these also occur as we age, especially as we enter the later years of adult life only to discover parts of ourselves life itself has taken away or reserved until now. Women who have spent the first decades of their adult lives raising a family or caring for a home may eventually discover unused gifts of academic inquiry or musical creation or service beyond their families, as Lillian Carter did at sixty-eight when she joined the Peace Corps. And men pushed to excel and to shut down their emotions may start opening closed doors and crossing thresholds into affective areas they have not entered until now. These too fall under the counsel to find out what belongs to whom and give it back.

Finally, there are two family situations that are a direct concern of Jubilee justice. Grace Harding, director of the Office for Persons with Disabilities in the Diocese of Pittsburgh, drew my attention to the first. Listening to me a decade ago as I delivered one of the first lectures I ever gave on Jubilee, she reminded me that the words of Isaiah and of Jesus in citing the Jubilee were not only, not even primarily, metaphorical. "Sight to the blind" means precisely and especially that: attending to those with the inability to see. Then Harding pointed out that those texts also refer to the proclamation of hearing for the deaf, and ramps, wide doorways, and accessible bathrooms for those who must use wheelchairs. These persons demand primary Jubilee attention, as do their parents and the rest of their families.

The other situation is the family made up of the widow and her fatherless children. My brother and I have some experience here: as the small children of a mother widowed after only ten short years of marriage, Tom and I knew something of the isolation, loneliness, and fear that the presence of sudden death brings and much of the trauma and bruising it can carry. Amazingly, we also knew Jubilee through the Jewish family who lived next door. Toward us, they lived the prescriptions of Torah fully and explicitly. Throughout my childhood they remembered us and cared for us through gifts of food, time, friendship, laughter, and prayer.

A Coda on Mourning

A surprising, although not unexpected, reaction often occurs as people begin finding out what belongs to whom and giving it back. They begin to mourn, although their reasons for mourning may differ. Sometimes the mourning is the natural response to the sobering corrective of suffering. Sometimes it is the natural response to the inexplicable loss accompanying the pain of the world. Sometimes it is the response to recognizing we are entering the pathos of God. And sometimes it is the resistance that accompanies the realization that we—and our possessions—must decrease if justice is to increase.

At other times our mourning is a passage through the stages learned from Elizabeth Kubler-Ross, who outlines a movement from denial to anger to bargaining to depression to acceptance, a movement that seems to take up residence within us.[27] If it does, the anger that is part of the mourning rhythm can be instructive. Theologian Beverly Harrison has written that anger signals attention to our awareness that all is not right with the world, and so it can be an ally. She extols the power of anger in the work of love, and in the work of justice.[28]

Sometimes our mourning has physical manifestations. It can include the characteristics that Erich Lindemann discovered in interviewing survivors and bereaved after the Coconut Grove nightclub in Boston burned in 1942.[29] This was a flash fire that left 492 dead in less than an hour, and those who were left manifested similar reactions: a disconcerting lack of warmth, somatic distress (pains in the stomach), preoccupation with the image of what had been lost, guilt, disorganized patterns of conduct, and the feeling one no longer fits. These same responses can appear as we take on the work of Jubilee.

Some would unthinkingly label these symptoms aberrant. But if we grieve the loss in the world, if we are in bodily distress due to its poisons, and if we feel we are out of place and no longer fit, we may be acting as the sanest ones of all, in a planet gone mad through acquisition.

Indeed, this may explain why we sometimes experience our mourning as endless. Although we know it is possible to get "stuck" in mourning, the sheer immensity of the world's grief and need bogs us down, and the heaviness may not lift until, mysteriously, we embrace mourning as a natural and necessary component of Jubilee justice and take it into ourselves.

Our precise relation to mourning, however, really does not matter, for once a person or a community or a nation mourns truly, its hands no longer clutch and it becomes free. Those free hands symbolize the ability to give back and return, as well as the power to let go. And once a person or community or nation has learned to find out what belongs to whom and give it back, it is itself released. It is set free *by* Jubilee justice and *toward* Jubilee justice into the vocation of proclaiming Jubilee throughout a broken world.

For Further Reflection and Conversation

1. Where do you find the themes of liberation, connectedness, suffering, imagination, and repair of the world occurring in the traditions of Jubilee justice?

2. What does it mean to say Jubilee is a curriculum of religious education? How might a curriculum be considered just?

3. Two forms of spirituality are described in this chapter. Where do you see them reflected in today's society? Why and how is the second more representative of Jubilee teaching than the first? How can we make the first more representative?

4. How, in today's world, is Jubilee justice a reflection of the pathos of God?

5. Five guidelines toward economic justice are presented in this chapter. How can they be made practical for you personally, as well as for the wider society?

6. How might religious educators be aware of ways that Jubilee justice can have an impact on families? What practices might help?

7. For what do you need to mourn personally, socially, and politically so that Jubilee justice may triumph?

6

Sing a New Song:
The Canticle of Jubilation

Prelude

On a recent Sunday in New York, I walked to the subway and boarded the D train as it headed north, away from our home in Greenwich Village. I was going to a bilingual mass held regularly at Our Lady of Victory, a Catholic parish in the South Bronx. Over the previous year-and-a-half I'd been working with a team from the parish on a religious education project, but our meetings were either on weekday evenings or Friday–Saturday overnights. This time, however, I traveled during a late Sunday morning because I wanted to take part in the liturgy with a group of men and women who'd become my friends and to pray with their English-speaking African American and Spanish-speaking Latino American co-parishioners. My anticipation was sweetened because the liturgy was to include a celebration of the first Holy Communion of twenty-four parishioners—most of them children—and a welcome feast for those adults baptized at the recent Easter Vigil.

I arrived as the entrance procession was moving down the main aisle, lucky to get a seat in the already packed church. I joined the hymn that the two choirs and numerous instrumental musicians were leading, adding my voice, my clapping hands, and my tapping feet to the words and music echoing against the walls and ceiling of the small church:

> Aleluya, Aleluya, es la Fiesta del Señor.
> Aleluya, Aleluya, El Señor Resucito.

> *Ya no hay miedo, ya no hay muerte;*
>   *ya no hay penas que llorar;*
> *Porque Cristo Sigue vivo, la esperanza abierta está.[1]*

The ancient liturgy had begun, new again as always and filled on this particular morning with the joy of the families who were there with children and grandchildren, pressing ever more closely against one another as time and again we paused in the ceremony so that people who were standing could find seats. Throughout the next hour-and-a-half I was caught up in a great symphony of prayer and song as we alternated between English and Spanish, my pale face an anomaly in a richness of black and brown and tan. It had been a long time since I'd prayed with such joy or sung with such abandon. Like everyone around me, I was engaged in gratitude, jubilation, and gladness as we sang, "Holy, Holy, Holy; Santo, Santo, Santo; Hosanna, Hosanna, Hosanna!"

Even while this was happening, two things were obvious to me. First, the prayer was real and people felt it. Reflecting on the experience a week later, I remembered something Dietrich Bonhoeffer had said during his time at New York's Union Theological Seminary, before he returned home to Germany and martyrdom by the Nazis. Bonhoeffer had commented that while in New York, the most vital and vibrant worship he'd experienced came when he prayed in black churches. I discovered something similar that morning as prayer rose from people who, though they knew hardship and need, welcomed the stranger in their midst, and joyfully praised the risen Christ.

And second, their prayer could not be contained by the spoken word. It *had* to erupt in song, in movement, in rhythm. It needed the flute and the organ, the trumpet and the cymbals. It needed not only to *say* but to *be* the words of Psalm 150: Praise God in the sanctuary, in the mighty firmament. Praise God, with trumpet sound, with lute and harp, with tambourine and dance, with strings and pipe. Praise God. Let everything that breathes praise God.

I begin the final chapter of *Proclaim Jubilee!* with this account because in making the Jubilee journey over the past several years, I have learned the integral connection between jubilation, Jubilee's last tradition, and song. Invariably, as I have traveled to teach or to lead workshops on Jubilee, someone will ask me if I know a particular piece of Jubilee music. When I don't, they introduce me to the piece, often to several. People have taught me Taizé music: canons such as "Jubilate Deo" and "Jubilate, Servite"; ostinato chorales such as "Laudate Dominum" and "Laudate Omnes Gentes"; joyous "Alleluias"; and praises such as "Psallite Deo" and "Psallite Domino."[2]

The songs and hymns I've learned also include Jim and Jean Strathdee's *Jubilee* collection, where the title song introduces the Jubilee traditions:

> *Once in ev'ry fifty year cycle,*
> *There must be a time of liberty.*
> *Slaves are released and their land is returned . . .*

—"with the trumpets sounding" as the first verse puts it, "with God's people crying," as the second verse recalls, and finally, as the third verse swells, "with God's justice proclaiming." What the people are sounding, crying, and proclaiming is

> *JUBILEE! Let the slave and the captive go free*
> *JUBILEE! Save the land and return it to me*
> *JUBILEE! Let people stand in their dignity*
> *In the year of God's Jubilee.*[3]

Still another Jubilee song is "Flowers Will Bloom in the Desert," by Walter Farquharson and Ron Klusmeier. Its four verses are particularly reminiscent of Isaiah 61, including such prophecies as "The hungry will feed at the banquet," "The blinded be able to see," and "All captives will walk out of prisons, surprised at their call to be free." Each time, the prophecies issue in a glorious refrain that promises:

> *Flowers will bloom in the desert,*
> *Captives walk free.*
> *These promises, God, you have given,*
> *Your people have nurtured this dream.*[4]

The music I have learned in these ways also offers an implicit response to one of the most frequently asked questions concerning the Jubilee. Usually the question is posed either as "But has the Jubilee ever been *tried*?" or, in more extreme form, as "Why *hasn't* the Jubilee ever been tried?" The response apparent in the music I've collected—that jubilation and festivity alone are not enough to bring about Jubilee wholeness—is especially evident in the Strathdee collection, which includes, under the rubric of *Jubilee,*

such songs as "In Defense of Creation"[5] (as in "let the land lie fallow"), "What Does the Lord Require?"[6] (as in "to do justice and
love kindness and walk humbly with your God"), and "Look Beyond the Refugee"[7] (as in "heavy loans from the big world banks,
backed up by terror, guns and tanks," keep the profits rolling back
to the big money, not to the refugees).

In other words, the response to whether the Jubilee has or hasn't
been tried is either "Only some of its traditions have been tried"—
such as resting the land or holding a feast—or "Only parts of particular traditions have been tried"—such as returning *some* land or
releasing *some* detainees (as in the recent opening of U.S. gates to
Cuban but not to Haitian children).[8] The full Jubilee must include
the practice of all its traditions among all people and is fulfilled only
when resting the land, forgiveness, freedom, and justice join jubilation in singing a new song.

With this prelude and preliminary statement of the wholeness
Jubilee demands, we can turn to jubilation, the last Jubilee tradition. First I look at a final set of Jubilee particulars, including the
meaning of the word *jubilee* and its connection with jubilation;
some of the peoples known for proclaiming Jubilee; and the reasons they do so. I conclude the book with an example of how the
process of jubilation might be celebrated as a liturgical form whose
rhythm moves from proclamation to repentance to listening to
thanksgiving to commissioning.

Meanings of Jubilee

Most people in our world are aware of the *modern* meaning of
jubilee. Popularly, the word signifies an occasion to remember and
to celebrate the anniversary of an auspicious event or significant
day, usually after a long period of time, whether that event is national or global, personal or familial. With joy and exultation we
remember the ending of war, the declaration of peace, the founding or liberating of nations. We also remember the establishment
of businesses, community organizations, or religious congregations that have served succeeding generations and continue into
our times as life-giving institutions. We commemorate the bonding
of a couple in a marriage that has endured or the birthday of a person who has achieved the fullness of fifty—or sixty—or eighty

years. These remembrances invariably include song, festivity, parade, and an outpouring of the kind of joy dictated by the counsel to "call the sabbath a delight" (Isa. 58:13). Known as the Sabbath of Sabbaths, Jubilee is such an occasion.

Jubilee's *ancient* meaning, however, remains the genesis and the foundation for this better-known and more popular understanding, even when celebrants are unaware of it. Etymologically, Jubilee's meaning may come from the Hebrew verb *ybl,* which signifies release, especially from debt,[9] although it is far more usual to find experts citing *yobel* as the foundation of the word. *Yobel* is the Hebrew term for a ram's horn or trumpet sounded in a public arena. That reverberating trumpet heralds celebration, music, and song.

With literal exactness, the original biblical teaching introduces this final Jubilee tradition: "You shall count off seven weeks of years, seven times seven years, so that the period of seven weeks of years gives forty-nine years. Then you shall have the trumpet sounded loud; . . . you shall have the trumpet sounded throughout all your land. And you shall hallow the fiftieth year. . . . For it is a jubilee; it shall be holy to you" (Lev. 25:8–9; 12a).

In our time, the year 2000 provides a preeminent occasion for Jubilee as it inaugurates the third millennium of the common era. We have explored this in previous chapters, especially in chapter 1.

But we have also explored the poetic, metaphoric, and spiritual force of Jubilee. And now, as we listen carefully to the command to sound the trumpet, we find still another meaning sedimented in it, one that is deeply personal. Recalling that the "land" in Jubilee always includes the land that we are, the words "you shall have the trumpet sounded throughout *all your land. . . .* For *it* is a jubilee" suggest that we ourselves are Jubilee land.[10] The first four Jubilee traditions have already taught us that not only is every fiftieth year a Jubilee, so is all of life, if we permit it to be. This teaching confirms and extends that, becoming a guide for every person every day and saying, "It—your existence—is a Jubilee. All the days of your life shall be holy to you."

Practitioners of Jubilee

Nations celebrate Jubilees, and some have a history of jubilarian practice. In Great Britain at the end of the nineteenth century, for example, Queen Victoria's sixtieth anniversary as monarch was revered as a year of Jubilee, and the celebration, with its pomp and glitter and ceremony, is still remembered in England.

At the end of the twentieth century, other nations, notably in Central and Latin America, are calling attention to contemporary Jubilee possibilities out of histories of struggle and oppression. These nations—and their advocates elsewhere—call for a Jubilee era of release from debt, freedom from conditions of bondage, and redistribution of wealth. As a result of liberation movements in our world, these political and prophetic dimensions of Jubilee are more widely known than they have been in previous centuries.

Religious institutions also hold regular Jubilees. Women and men in religious orders, for example, periodically acknowledge both corporate and personal fullness of years. Religious orders' Jubilees are often celebrations of an order's founding, centuries ago in the case of Benedictines (529 C.E.), Franciscans (1209 C.E.), Dominicans (1233 C.E.), or Sisters of Saint Joseph (1650 C.E.), more recently in the case of the Sisters of Mercy or Maryknoll.

Vowed members of these orders also personally observe their profession anniversaries after twenty-five or fifty years, and sometimes even longer than that, even as they remember the orders' and the members' involvement in Sabbath, forgiveness, liberty, and justice. Among other religious institutions celebrating Jubilee, I have already cited the Evangelical Lutheran Church in America, Pax Christi, and individual parishes and local congregations that are finding ways to practice Jubilee as part of their own ecclesial history.

I have also cited the current *papacy* as a practitioner, although the Catholic Church's relation to Jubilee is actually very old, going back at least to 1300 C.E. when Pope Boniface VIII declared a Jubilee year directed to remission of the penal consequences of sin. This remission could be obtained through disciplines such as pilgrimage, almsgiving, fasting, and other works of mercy that continue as modern religious practices. At first the papacy proclaimed Jubilee years only every hundredth year, but in time a papal Jubilee could occur on a fiftieth anniversary, a twenty-fifth, or a thirty-third. Today, Rome even declares an "extraordinary" Jubilee year for individual countries or cities at times other than these and often designates the length of such Jubilees for periods other than an entire year.

John Paul II, however, has returned to the biblical Jubilee traditions as has no pope in recent memory. In doing so, as at least one journalist has noted, he has seriously complicated the stereotype of himself as a reactionary "intent on consolidating the past rather than facing the future."[11] In the program outlined in the document titled "Reflections on the Great Jubilee of the Year 2000," released in 1994, he proposed a serious examination of conscience for the church directed toward confessing the sins, errors, and even crimes committed by its representatives and in its name over the last two thousand years. As other occasions when the pope has spoken to this issue indicate, these might include repentance for the burning at the stake of Jan Hus and the martyrdom of other Reformers;[12] the involvement of the church in the slave trade; the church's failure to bring justice to the indigenous peoples of the Americas; the excesses of the Crusades; the Inquisition; and the practices of anti-Semitism that contributed to the Shoah.[13]

Another suggestion linked to Jubilee is the pope's call for a joint assembly to be held on Mount Sinai by leaders of Christianity, Judaism, and Islam, directed toward renouncing all violence among those who share a common ancestry in an attempt to put aside old antagonisms. In addition, the pope is calling for a pan-Christian reunion at Bethlehem and Jerusalem in collaboration with the World Council of Churches and the Great Council of Orthodoxy. In each of these proposals, one hears the music of the great Jubilee themes, especially forgiveness, liberation, and justice.

Still, as I have sought to discover adherents of Jubilee in modern times, I have found no people more involved with living the Jubilee than *African Americans*. Doing an initial library study, for example, I found that most of the works in the catalog under "Jubilee" resonated with the lives and spirits of black people. Among these works were *What Was Freedom's Price?* a collection that begins with the Jubilee emancipation of 1865 and then explores the impact of Reconstruction on African Americans; *Frederick Douglass' Civil War: Keeping Faith with Jubilee*; and *The Fires of Jubilee: Nat Turner's Fierce Rebellion*.[14]

I also found Margaret Walker's 1966 novel *Jubilee*, the story of her great-grandmother's life before, during, and after the Civil War, which has sold over one million copies and illustrates the many facets of Jubilee through a classic, ancestral story. One of the numerous creative elements in the work is Walker's constant use of songs throughout the text, many of them spirituals. Every chapter begins with at least a snatch of song ("Every nigger's gwine to own a mule, Jubili, Jubilo! / Every nigger's gwine to own a mule / And live like Adam in the golden rule / And send his chillun to the white-folk's school / In the year of Jubilo!").[15] In fact, as if to signal the importance of song to Jubilee, Walker has noted the words of the traditional Negro spiritual "Jubilee" immediately after the title page:

> *We are climbing Jacob's ladder,*
> *We are climbing Jacob's ladder,*
> *We are climbing Jacob's ladder,*
>   *for the year of Jubilee!*
>
> *Every round goes higher, higher,*
> *Every round goes higher, higher,*
> *Every round goes higher, higher,*
>   *to the year of Jubilee.*
>
> *Do you think I'll make a soldier?*
> *Do you think I'll make a soldier?*
> *Do you think I'll make a soldier,*
>   *in the year of Jubilee?*

The attention of black people to Jubilee's power should come as no surprise. Not only do African Americans preserve in their own experience a history of the slavery and suffering and longing for liberation that the Jubilee sought to address, they also embody its major tenets. If we reflect on the interplay of biblical strength, appreciation of Sabbath, passion for freedom and justice, and capacity for forgiveness, evident especially in today's black churches, we see this interplay modeled in the lives of African Americans to an extent that few others can equal.

Reasons for Celebrating Jubilee

Why celebrate a Jubilee today? This question has a number of other renderings: Why hold a Jubilee? Why be one? Why insist on Jubilee as a spirituality? Why make it a curriculum of religious education? There is even a rendering of this question as "Why, given the terror and bloodshed and evil in the world, would *anyone* hold a Jubilee?" I hope that by now readers of this book are answering these questions for themselves and their communities, persuaded that the power of Jubilee and Jubilee's God can recreate lives, societies, historical eras. My hunch is that if they are, the following is part of their response:

1. We celebrate Jubilee today because the times demand it. The force of a final decade, the end of a century, and the close of a millennium contribute to the urgency, just as these endings turn into new beginnings. New beginnings traditionally are times of possibility and times of decision, making the time itself a significant factor directing us to Jubilee celebration.

2. We celebrate Jubilee today as a response to the challenges with which the twentieth century leaves us and the twenty-first century confronts us. Jubilee is one very significant way in which we can answer these challenges. As I tried to show in chapter 1, these questions include the following: Where does liberation claim us? How shall we practice connectedness? What demands does global suffering make on us? What artistic powers do we possess? What contribution will we make to the task of repairing the world?

   As their adherents are teaching us today, the Jubilee traditions are profound religious responses to these questions. As part of our spiritual, moral, and religious heritage, we have received the power that lies in Sabbath, in forgiveness, in release of captives, in justice, and in jubilation. The power in each is not discrete or disconnected from the others, however. Instead, Jubilee power arises from the practice of all of these traditions in concert, with the exercise of one activating the exercise of the others.

3. We celebrate Jubilee today to acknowledge that the world continues to be charged with the grandeur of God and that the Holy Spirit continues to brood over the bent world with warm breast and with ah! bright wings. Proclaiming a Jubilee is an act of faith, an act of hope, and an act of conviction that grace, goodness, and holiness exist, even though none of them has triumphed fully. The festive jubilarian tradition makes particular sense in this context, for it says that despite brokenness, there is Sabbath quiet; despite brother murdering brother, there is forgiveness; despite massive inequality, there is prophetic justice. Despite slaughter, our world lurches toward Bethlehem, where a new world aches to be born.

   The hope that such birth is possible in our often sorry world receives regular confirmation. Not only is the Berlin Wall demolished, Germany is reunified. Not only is Nelson Mandela free, he is president of South Africa. And in the course of only one recent year, the United Nations has celebrated yet another environmental Sabbath out of love for the land, even as the Children's Defense Fund has led millions in a Children's Sabbath out of concern for the youngest in our midst. Great Britain and Northern Ireland have begun discussions on ending the violence in the tortured counties of Ulster. Jean-Bertrand Aristide has returned to Haiti, and Port-au-Prince has taken time out for dancing in the streets. Jimmy Carter continues to wage peace and, with Habitat for Humanity, to build homes for the poor. And Israel and Jordan, in their promise that they "will share water," offer a sacramental symbol that where sin and terror have abounded, grace abounds even more.

4. Finally, as we shall discover in the jubilation liturgy to follow, we celebrate Jubilee today to give thanks to the Giver of all good gifts. We celebrate Jubilee as an act of gratitude. I will return to this as part of the process of jubilation, but I name gratitude here as a central reason for *why* we take part in Jubilee, prior to considering *how*. Our canticle is incomplete if it stops at "Jubilate," which is translated as "Give thanks and glory and praise." It must go on to "Jubilate *Deo*"—"Give thanks and glory and praise to the *Giver*." Before the Mystery of Being itself, no matter how we name this Mystery, we must *give* thanks and we must *be* thanks, or perish from ingratitude.

As a people, the Hebrews, ancient and modern, never forgot this. Even when captured by the conquering armies of Nebuchadnezzar, who exiled them to Babylon, even in the ghettoes and in the camps, they praised and gave thanks to their God, Yahweh. They created the biblical book called Psalms, where characteristic opening verses are as follows:

> I thank you, Yahweh, with all my heart;
> I sing praise to you before the gods.
>   (Ps. 138:1)

and

> I will praise you, Yahweh, with my whole heart;
> I will tell of all your marvelous works.
>   (Ps. 9:1)

and

> I give thanks to you, Yahweh, for you are good,
> your love is everlasting.
>   (Ps. 118:1)[16]

As the centuries piled up, the Hebrews acted on the counsel of the Talmud that in every generation, at every Passover feast, at every weekly Sabbath, and during every seventh year, each would regard herself or himself as though she or he had just emerged from Egypt and, in remembering, give thanks. Such is the tradition that reminds us why we celebrate Jubilee and why, to be complete, our song must be "Jubilate Deo."

The Process of Jubilation: Jubilee's Liturgical Ritual

As we become convinced of the need for Jubilee in our times, we also become aware of the need for forms to fashion it. In this concluding section, I offer a liturgical form that embodies Jubilee practice. Paying homage to the truth that, in essence, Jubilee is a great and majestic ritual, in the same way that living and loving and dying are rituals, I suggest jubilation as our guide, since in addition to being Jubilee's celebratory center it is already, at least implicitly, a hallowed model for religious ceremony in many communities and communions.

Like all rituals, Jubilee's is made up of specific steps, rhythm, and aesthetic form. These can be discerned by contemplating Leviticus 25 and prayerfully meditating on Isaiah 61 and Luke 4:16–20. These texts reveal the "how" of jubilation, its process and its practice, which necessarily include Sabbath, forgiveness, freedom, and justice, even as they sum these up.

What follows is one way of putting this process together, in a ritual intended as both catalyst and model for those who want to design similar forms more closely fitting their own contexts. The form includes five elements regularly highlighted in any process of jubilation and familiar in most liturgies and services of worship. The form begins with *proclamation,* or announcement; continues with a period of *repentance* and *forgiveness;* pauses for *waiting upon the Holy;* sings out a song of *thanksgiving;* and issues finally in a *commissioning* to works that serve freedom and justice.

This liturgy may be held in the space of an hour, although that is difficult and a day or a week is better. It is even more aesthetically appropriate to hold it over an entire year—even two—which would be more consonant with Jubilee teaching. It may also be held—and held up—as the work of a lifetime, nourishing those who are answering the call to Jubilee.

Proclamation

The first element in a jubilation liturgy draws on the command to gather up the times; the minutes, the hours, and the years. Then, on a day the community chooses, the trumpet sounds and the announcement is made, proclaiming a Jubilee.

The chosen day of proclamation will differ in different circumstances.[17] But essential to this first part of the liturgy is proclaiming the Jubilee as a festival for all. The biblical text makes it clear that the announcement and the proclamation are of liberty "throughout the land." Therefore, Jubilee is announced as a political and prophetic event.

Both André Trocmé and John Howard Yoder stress jubilation's—and Jubilee's—political character. Yoder, commenting on Luke 4:14 and the verses that follow, remarks that Jesus' initial message was in the same words as those used by John the Baptist, "The kingdom of God is at hand; repent and believe in the good news." Yoder goes on to say that the language of "kingdom" and "gospel" (evangel) is chosen from the political realm.[18] He argues further that Jesus' selection of this vocabulary would be out of place if his own proclamation had differed from John's.

Although most people know that *kingdom* is a political term, the ordinary reader of the Bible is usually far less aware that *gospel,* or *evangel,* is also a political term. *Gospel* means not any old welcome report but the kind of publicly important proclamation that is worth sending with a runner—a *kēryx,* or "herald"—and worth celebrating when the runner arrives.[19]

So, too, the news of Jubilee. Like Sabbath, its proclamation is toward ceasing ordinary labor and finding expression in singing, feasting, and celebration. And although, as the ritual starts, we are guided by songs of the soul that express and symbolize *recreation* in community, the proclamation holds proclaimers and receivers to further involvement. Both must acknowledge they are heralding a new creation, a new world and a new social order, where death and mourning shall be no more. In this the announcement resonates with another biblical proclamation, the one in the book of Revelation that testifies:

> And I heard a loud voice from the throne saying,
>   "See, the home of God is among mortals.
>   [God] will dwell with them as their God;
>   they will be [God's] peoples,

and God . . . will be with them;
[God] will wipe every tear from their eyes.
Death will be no more;
mourning and crying and pain will be no more,
for the first things have passed away."

(Rev. 21:3–4)

Repentance and Forgiveness

In both Jewish and Christian liturgical tradition and practice, acts of repentance and forgiveness have always been given pride of place. Often that place has been at a liturgy's beginning, or as in the case of Lent leading on to Easter, in preparation for the great feast. So, too, in the ritual of jubilation. The gathering of a community to hear Jubilee proclaimed proceeds now to acknowledge the community members' failures, before one another and before God.

Ancient hymns can initiate this step in the Jubilee liturgy: "Kyrie, eleison; Christe, eleison; Kyrie, eleison"—Lord, have mercy; Christ, have mercy; Lord, have mercy. Or together a community can repeat such words as:

We confess to the God of our mothers and fathers,
and we confess to our brothers and sisters,
that we have sinned through our own fault,
in our thoughts and in our words,
in what we have done,
and in what we have failed to do.

Then we can follow the words with silence, as we reflect on what we have done and failed to do, especially as communities and especially—if this applies to us—as privileged people, often unaware of our privilege.

Chapter 3 of this book provides a formula for this part of the liturgy. There the practice of forgiveness includes willingness to answer the question "Forgive what, and ask forgiveness of what?"—remembering especially our debts and sins and omissions in the social as well as in the interpersonal arena. We also need to pause and to answer the question "Forgive and be forgiven by whom?"—concentrating on asking forgiveness from our families, our intimates, and the people our people have harmed.

In addition, the question "Ask forgiveness of whom?" includes those we might have aided but did not and those who have been harmed in our name—the so-called enemies who have been adversaries or on "the other side"—in wars our country has fought abroad, as well as closer to home: on the other side of town or the other side of our family. We are even required to remember our responsibility to those impossible to forgive and to decide on the forms such responsibility might take.

And then we are directed to repent. Often an ordinary liturgy is too brief a time to engage in the repentance demanded by Jubilee—another argument for this being a liturgy of some length. It is not out of the question to give time to this work over several years, as 2000 approaches and after it arrives, perhaps following the example offered earlier of searching history and tradition and preparing to lament and to ask forgiveness for our own and our church's sins over centuries.

For a community taking part in such a ritual, this might mean a movement toward conversation across religious lines, across racial lines, across ethnic lines, and across other barriers such as age, class, and sexual orientation, both within our communities and beyond their borders. The *New York Times* recently reported on one such conversation among 150 members of one family, the Alstons, who came together in Inez, North Carolina, for a family reunion. Descendants of slaves and of slave owners, half the family is black and half is white.[20] They had gathered to find out who they were and to open their lives to one another. Out of such meetings, once trust is established and often when tears are permitted and music sung, Jubilee forgiveness can emerge.

When forgiveness is asked for and granted, the ritual performance of this step can conclude, as we seek the assistance of the entire communion of saints through petitions such as:

And we ask the entire heavenly court,
We ask Abraham and Sarah,
David and Michel, Uriah and Bathsheba,
Ruth and Naomi and Orpah;
We ask blessed Mary and Joseph, her husband,
We ask the holy apostles Peter and Paul,
We ask our ancestors and the ancestors of those we have harmed,
We ask the wind and the stars, the earth and the water,
We ask all the angels and saints,
even as we ask you [present] who are our brothers and sisters,
to pray for us to the God of all mercies.

Finally, we can respond to one another:

> May the God of forgiveness and compassion
> pardon you all your sins,
> and bring you to everlasting life. Amen.

Waiting upon the Holy

The tradition of waiting upon the Holy by pausing to let the land lie fallow is never far from the jubilarian imagination. As part of a Jubilee liturgy, and placed at its center, the particular power of this step lies in its fostering the conditions necessary for listening—the "centering down" that Quakers speak of—in order to wait upon that One variously invoked as the Holy, the Mystery at the core of the universe, Jehovah, or the Creator Spirit—the One some of us call God or the Great Mother and others refer to as "beyond all names"—so we might hear what the Holy requires of us as persons and as communities. We listen so that we might find ways to proclaim liberty throughout the land and to search out what belongs to whom, in order to give it back.

As this century ends and another begins, people of many religious paths—even of none—have begun to observe regular periods of such stillness as part of their personal spirituality, pausing daily for twenty- or thirty-minute periods not to address but to be addressed by and to *listen* to the Holy. Through such practices, they have become attuned to hearing the Holy not only in human voices but in the cries of the earth and the headlines of the newspaper. They have also become attuned to hearing the Holy in the silence.

Jubilation, however, is a *communal* tradition; therefore, at this point in the Jubilee liturgy, persons bring the power such practice develops in their private lives to listening *together* in community, as a corporate task where one another's presence is a source of strength. They wait. They cultivate stillness. Sometimes they sit for a month; sometimes for six. Always they make this step central, neither rushing it nor forgoing it. Sabbath candles lighted, they refuse to be anxious. Instead, together they engage in emptying their minds and hearts of busyness, resting in contemplative silence so that the Holy might break through.

During such periods, it is not always easy to be completely silent. Many religious communities are so talkative that they do not realize they are blocking the entrance of the Holy into their midst by speaking about it too much. Others are so busy doing what they believe is God's work that they do not create opportunities to check in with God to make sure. Still others are immune to God-infection; they stave off the fiery vocation God demands of them by domesticating the Creator Spirit, too easily assuming they already know the Spirit's nature and the kinds of requests it seeks to make of them.

We should hope to be strengthened, centered, and healed by the Holy, true. But we should also expect to be stunned and dazed by it, jolted and astounded, something that is less likely unless we prepare for it by waiting and listening. So in this part of the liturgy, as we wait upon the presence of the Holy, let us be—as Annie Dillard has written—"sufficiently sensible of conditions" and have some idea of the sort of power we are invoking or waiting upon. Come into community to listen for it; let us recognize that it can change our lives. Dillard suggests a way to make this happen, as she continues, "Ushers should issue life preservers and signal flares; they should lash us to our pews. For the sleeping god may wake someday and take offense, or the waking god may draw us out to where we can never return."[21]

Thanksgiving

When God arrives, however, whether sleeping or waking, that arrival provokes a response. Having engaged in what Buddhists call "mindfulness," partnered one another in communal repentance, and discerned the nature of our call, we are now ready to answer it. Moving into that response, we are no longer silent. Instead, because this is a liturgy informed by jubilation, we find ourselves singing a song of gratitude, a psalm of thanks, a chorus of "Hallelujah." As we do, we discover that the thanksgiving that provoked us to create this liturgy is actually its undersong, its essential music. Like the community with whose liturgy this chapter began, we too are impelled to sing, "Holy, Holy, Holy; Santo, Santo, Santo; Hosanna, Hosanna, Hosanna."[22]

"Gratitude is the virtue that all devout women and men share," writes philosopher Louis Dupré. "The Buddhist as well as the Benedictine monk *thanks* all day long independent of personal mood or feeling. At the end of the day, monks sing their thanks for whatever the day has brought—pleasure, boredom or pain. . . . Every day is Godgiven, and as such, good."[23]

Ironically, the mystery of brokenness and the mystery of gratitude are inextricably connected. The impulses that move us to lessen injustice and wrong come not only because we have listened. They also come as a direct result of realizing that the gifts of life belong to everyone.[24] When we decide to confront brutality, racism, or any of the wrongs in our world—as Jubilee impels us to do—we do so because we have a prior conviction. Peace, employment opportunities, health, food, and education are universal gifts. There's a fault line in the universe, however, that prevents those gifts from reaching all but a privileged minority of the world's people. Some call the fault line evil; theologians call it sin.

But theologians also teach that where sin abounds, grace abounds even more. Goodness already exists in our world—to believe otherwise is to give in to despair—but it is partial goodness, incomplete goodness. The fitting human response to evil, and the way in which we can fulfill our potential for goodness, is to accept our responsibility to all earth's creatures and try to repair the inequality and deprivation that prevent things being as they ought.

Accepting this responsibility, we need to recognize the ordinary and pervasive gifts of our own lives, including the forgiveness and freedom and justice that are already ours. The prophetic action toward which we now move emerges ineluctably from the prior steps of waiting upon the Holy and then genuflecting our thanksgiving to it. Our grateful hearts finally impel us into the practice of freedom and into tasks that lessen the injustice in our world. Anticipating these, our liturgy enters its final step, where we signal acceptance of the commission to proclaim Jubilee throughout the world.

Commissioning and Sending Forth

In my imagination, I see jubilation's last step taking place in one enormous gathering of interlocking circles. In circle after circle, men and women and children join hands together, singing, praying, crying, proclaiming. As the music softens, several of their number—perhaps the eldest man and woman and the youngest children in the circle—chant the ancient Jubilee counsels whose melodies permeate this tradition:

> You shall have the trumpet sounded loud
> throughout all your land . . . .

> You shall hallow the fiftieth year. . . .
>
> You shall proclaim liberty throughout the land
> to all its inhabitants. . . .
>
> It shall be a jubilee for you . . . . .
>
> You shall return, every one of you, to your prop-
> erty and every one of you to your people . . . .
>
> It is a jubilee; it shall be holy to you.

This chant initiates jubilation's last moments, when all the people in all the circles name a specific Jubilee action they will take (of Sabbath, forgiveness, freedom, justice, jubilation).[25] The naming is part of a great litany and draws forth the assurance through which the assembly itself commissions them. That assurance is promised with the words "Go forth and be a Jubilee. For we are your people."

In Jubilee teaching, once the trumpet sounds, the land rests, and the songs are sung, one thing remains. We are told to "return" to our people. We have already probed one meaning of this return with the tradition of freedom, as we learned we were free to go home, to remember, and to re-create. We have probed a second meaning with the tradition of justice. Now the commissioning of jubilation invites us to gather, in both of these, a return of handing over and restoring the gifts of God's good earth through responses that serve freedom, that serve justice. At the end, the only way to fulfill the Jubilee vocation is to extend the return to "our" people commanded by Jubilee to all people and to restore "our" place, Earth, to its rightful inheritance of clear water, clean air, and fruitful soil in every corner of the planet.

Anticipating this final step, I have been naming its vehicle as "works" that serve justice and freedom, and as "practices." Because these may suggest activity alone—doing, in contrast to being—I need to say that every community must commission *receptive* work as well as *active* work; sending its people forth to the not-doing of Sabbath as well as to the merciful doing of justice and liberation. We have no way of gauging whether lying on one's back in pain is any less valuable than feeding hungry people in re-creating a Jubilee world. So the sending forth is to both the simplicity and the grandeur of staying at one's post and doing one's best, wherever we find ourselves. Our work can be as ordinary as caring for our children and changing their diapers and as unusual as teaching fish-farming to India's rural poor. It can be as play-filled as a game of basketball and as serious as burying our dead. In this final step, naming the vocations that call us, we should expect them to be as varied as the stars.

That said, the vocations to which commissioning directs us rise from Jubilee itself. Some of us will be commissioned mainly as Sabbath people—not only in keeping it but in assisting the rest of the community to let the land lie fallow. Some will be agents of forgiveness—counselors, therapists, healers, penitents. Others will work to serve justice as students, teachers, ecologists, homemakers, money-raisers, or entrepreneurs of Camp Lemonade Stands. Others will practice Jubilee in the governmental arena, as policymakers and as executives. Still others will be jubilant artists: dancers and jugglers, sculptors and singers, poets and mimes.

But no matter where the going forth leads, it will have some distinguishing features. Boundary-crossing will be one: the work that returns us home will often send us far away. Risk-taking will be another, both the risk of doing too little and the risk of doing too much. Creativity—generating new ideas, new institutions, new lives—will be a third. Each will anoint us to the vocation of proclaiming Jubilee.

So as we join the circle, and as our turn comes to speak our intentions for the future, we need not be hesitant. Whatever we do and whoever we are, we are on a path toward repairing the world together. Believing the ever-present God of Jubilee is with us, we call out our Jubilee dreams and in response are strengthened by the majestic chorus that companions us in making them come true. This is the chorus that sings our commissioning with one mighty voice as, accompanied by the trumpet's sound, it proclaims over and over to all who have gathered, "Go forth and be a Jubilee. For we are your people."

For Further Reflection and Conversation

1. Where do you find the themes of liberation, connectedness, suffering, imagination, and repair of the world occurring in the tradition of jubilation?

2. What songs do you associate with Jubilee? Why would Jubilee be incomplete without song?

3. What have been occasions of jubilation in your life? What were some of the elements that made these times of Jubilee? Have the reasons for your gratitude changed from one Jubilee experience to the next?

4. What have been occasions of jubilation in the life of your family, religious tradition, nation? What do you remember of the festivity connected with them?

5. What do you think is the reason for the African American awareness of Jubilee? What might you learn from African American faith in the Jubilee?

6. If you were designing it, what would you include in a Jubilee liturgy that has not been mentioned in this chapter?

7. What vocation would you claim in the face of the assembly commissioning you to go forth and be Jubilee to the world?

Notes

1. Themes in a Century: Challenges for Jubilee

1. Maria Harris, *Jubilee Time: Celebrating Women, Spirit, and the Advent of Age* (New York: Bantam Books, 1995).

2. See Maria Harris, *Dance of the Spirit* (New York: Bantam Books, 1989), for a developed understanding of this meaning, esp. pp. 67ff.

3. Walter Brueggemann, "Voices of the Night—Against Justice," in Walter Brueggemann, Sharon Parks, and Thomas H. Groome, *To Act Justly, Love Tenderly, Walk Humbly: An Agenda for Ministers* (New York: Paulist Press, 1986), pp. 5–6.

4. See, for example, Carolyn Forché, ed., *Against Forgetting: Twentieth Century Poetry of Witness* (New York: W. W. Norton & Co., 1993).

5. Martin Buber, *Between Man and Man,* trans. Ronald Gregor Smith (London: Routledge & Kegan Paul, 1947), pp. 9, 10.

6. Christopher Fry, *A Sleep of Prisoners* (New York: Oxford University Press, 1951), pp. 47–48.

7. Gustavo Gutiérrez, *A Theology of Liberation* (Maryknoll, N.Y.: Orbis Books, 1973).

8. Robert McAfee Brown, "Kairos International: Call to Conversion," *Christian Century* (November 22, 1989): 1091.

9. Ibid.

10. Ibid.

11. Paulo Freire, *Pedagogy of the Oppressed* (New York: Herder & Herder, 1970). See also his *Education for Critical Consciousness* (New York: Seabury Press, 1973).

12. See Robert Wuthnow, *Sharing the Journey* (New York: Free Press, 1994), for a careful study of small groups.

13. Wendy Kaminer, *I'm Dysfunctional, You're Dysfunctional: The Recovery Movement and Other Self-Help Fashions* (Reading, Mass.: Addison-Wesley Publishing Co., 1992).

14. See Christopher Lasch, *The Culture of Narcissism: American Life in an Age of Diminishing Expectations* (New York: W. W. Norton & Co., 1978).

15. Antonio Machado, "Moral Proverbs and Folk Songs," in *Times Alone,* trans. Robert Bly (Middletown, Conn.: Wesleyan University Press, 1983), p. 147; quoted in Robert Bly, *Iron John* (Reading, Mass.: Addison-Wesley Publishing Co., 1990).

16. Alice Walker, *The Color Purple* (New York: Washington Square Press, 1982), p. 249.

17. Dennis Meadows, quoted in "Humanity Confronts Its Handiwork: An Altered Planet," *New York Times,* May 5, 1992, sec. C, p. 6.

18. Padraic O'Hare's reflection is found in the *Alternative Newsletter* 17, 3 (January 1991): 2–3. See also his *Busy Life, Peaceful Center* (Allen, Tex.: Thomas More/Tabor, 1995).

19. Thich Nhat Hanh, *Peace Is Every Step* (New York: Bantam Books, 1992), p. 95.

20. O'Hare, in *Alternative Newsletter* 17, 3:2–3.

21. Ernest Becker, *The Denial of Death* (New York: Free Press, 1973), p. 284.

22. The anecdote was reported to me by someone who heard it secondhand. I have been unable to trace it further.

23. Byars's immensely creative output is handled by the Michael Werner Gallery in New York; Baselitz has just had a major retrospective at the Guggenheim (June 1995); and Rubins is, by all accounts, the most striking contributor to the Whitney Biennial of 1995.

24. For Chilean and Zairean work, see Guy Brett, *Through Our Own Eyes* (Philadelphia: New Society Publishers, 1987). For Nicaraguan work, see Philip Scharper and Sally Scharper, eds., *The Gospel in Art by the Peasants of Solentiname* (Maryknoll, N.Y.: Orbis Books, 1984).

25. See Paul Ricoeur, "The Image of God and the Epic of Man," in *History and Truth* (Evanston, Ill.: Northwestern University Press, 1965), p. 127.

26. Susan Sontag, *On Photography* (New York: Dell Publishing Co., 1978), p. 18.

27. See Lewis Lapham's remarkable commentary on this event in "Notebook: Terms of Endearment," *Harper's,* September 1994, pp. 7–8.

28. Paul Gray, "Looking at Cataclysms," *Time,* August 1, 1994, p. 64.

29. Ibid.
30. William Butler Yeats, "A Prayer for Old Age," in *The Poems of W. B. Yeats: A New Edition,* ed. Richard J. Finneran (New York: Macmillan Publishing Co., 1983).
31. The definition is Suzanne Langer's; see her *Feeling and Form* (New York: Charles Scribner's Sons, 1953) and *Problems of Art* (New York: Charles Scribner's Sons, 1957).
32. See Douglas Johnston and Cynthia Sampson, eds., *Religion: The Missing Dimension of Statecraft* (New York: Oxford University Press, 1994).
33. I am indebted to my colleague Dr. Sherry Blumberg of Hebrew Union College in New York for introduction to the metaphor of *tikkun olam.* See also Judith Plaskow, *Standing Again at Sinai: Judaism from a Feminist Perspective* (San Francisco: Harper San Francisco, 1990) especially chap. 6, "Feminist Judaism and Repair of the World," pp. 211–38.
34. See Plaskow, *Standing Again at Sinai,* pp. 223–24, for development of this idea.

2. Let the Land Lie Fallow

1. Emilio Castro, *Your Kingdom Come* (Geneva: WCC, 1980); Mortimer Arias, "The Jubilee: A Paradigm for Mission Today," in *International Review of Mission* (Geneva: Commission on World Mission and Evangelism of WCC, January 1984), pp. 33–48; André Trocmé, *Jesus and the Nonviolent Revolution* (Scottdale, Pa.: Herald Press, 1983); John Howard Yoder, *The Politics of Jesus* (Grand Rapids: Wm. B. Eerdmans Publishing Co., 1972); Sharon H. Ringe, *Jesus, Liberation and the Biblical Jubilee* (Philadelphia: Fortress Press, 1985); Dorothee Soelle, "God's Economy and Ours: The Year of the Jubilee," in *God and Capitalism: A Prophetic Critique of Market Economy,* ed. J. Mark Thomas and Vern Visick (Madison, Wis.: A-R Editions, 1991), pp. 87–103.
2. See *National Catholic Reporter* (July 29, 1994): p. 8.
3. For information, contact ELCA Division for Congregational Ministries, 8765 West Higgins Road, Chicago, IL 60631.
4. Herman E. Daly, "A Biblical Economic Principle and the Steady-State Economy," *Epiphany Journal* 12 (winter 1992): 6–18; Alvin Schorr, *Jubilee for Our Times: A Practical Program for Income Equality* (New York: Columbia University Press, 1977).

5. See "New Evangelization: 1992 the Year of Grace of the Lord. The Bishops and Missionaries of Panama Propose the Celebration of a Continental Jubilee Year," *SEDOS Bulletin* (May 15, 1991): 139–41.

6. See Jerry Ryan, "The News That Didn't Fit," *Commonweal* (October 21, 1994): 6; and Desmond O'Grady, "The Perils of Penance," *Commonweal* (October 21, 1994): 7.

7. See Arthur Waskow, "From Compassion to Jubilee," *Tikkun* (March–April 1990): 78–81, and idem, "Sacred Earth, Sacred Earthling," *Gnosis* (fall 1994): 58–62; see also Richard Cartwright Austin, "Jubilee Now! The Political Necessity of the Biblical Call for Land Reform," *Sojourners* (June 1991): 26–30.

8. One such parish is Blessed Sacrament Catholic Community of Alexandria, Virginia, founded in 1946 and celebrating its Jubilee over the period of a year from September 1995 to September 1996.

9. See Yoder, *Politics of Jesus*, pp. 69–70. A *prosboul* (Greek for "an action formalized before the tribunal") was a document authorizing a creditor to transfer to a court the right to recover in his name a debt that the sabbatical or the Jubilee year otherwise might have canceled.

10. See J. Massyngbaerde Ford, *My Enemy Is My Guest: Jesus and Violence in Luke* (Maryknoll, N.Y.: Orbis Books, 1984); J. A. Sanders, "From Isaiah 61 to Luke 4," in *Christianity, Judaism and Other Greco-Roman Cults: Studies for Morton Smith at Sixty,* ed. Jacob Neusner, 4 vols. (Leiden: E. J. Brill, 1975).

11. For this introductory section, I am indebted to Walter C. Kaiser, Jr.'s opening comments in "The Book of Leviticus: Introduction, Commentary and Reflections," in *The New Interpreter's Bible* (Nashville: Abingdon Press, 1994), vol. 1, pp. 1170–71.

12. Quoted in Patricia Mische, "Parenting in a Hungry World," *New Catholic World* (Sept.–Oct. 1977): 238.

13. George E. Tinker, "Reading the Bible as Native Americans," in *The New Interpreter's Bible* (Nashville: Abingdon Press, 1994), vol. 1, p. 176.

14. In M. Sze, ed., *The Mustard Seed Garden Manual of Painting: A Facsimile* (Princeton, N.J.: Princeton University Press, 1978). I am indebted to Nathan A. Scott, Jr., for introduction to this work, as well as for his commentary on it in *The Broken Center: Studies on the Theological Horizon of Modern Literature* (New Haven, Conn.: Yale University Press, 1966), pp. 150–51.

15. Václav Havel, quoted in "The New Measure of Man," in *New York Times,* July 8, 1994, sec. C, p. 16.

16. Ibid.
17. Gerard Manley Hopkins, "God's Grandeur," in *A Hopkins Reader,* ed. John Pick (Garden City, N.Y.: Doubleday, 1966), pp. 47–48.
18. Annie Dillard, *Pilgrim at Tinker Creek* (New York: Bantam Books, 1974), p. 248.
19. Abraham Joshua Heschel, *The Earth Is the Lord's* and *The Sabbath* (New York: Harper & Row, 1951; reprint, 1962), p. 21.
20. Gabriel Marcel, *Philosophy of Existence* (New York: Philosophical Library, 1949), pp. 25–26.
21. Kosuke Koyama, *Three Mile an Hour God* (London: SCM Press, 1979), p. 5; see also the preface, p. ix.
22. See Samuel Terrien, *The Elusive Presence* (New York: Harper & Row, 1978), p. 3.
23. Ibid., p. 393.
24. In Samuel Bacchiocchi, "Remembering the Sabbath: The Creation-Sabbath in Jewish and Christian History," in Tamara C. Eskenazi, Daniel J. Harrington, and William H. Shea, eds., *The Sabbath in Jewish and Christian Traditions* (New York: Crossroad, 1991), p. 72.
25. Walter Brueggemann, "The Book of Exodus" in *The New Interpreter's Bible* (Nashville: Abingdon Press, 1994), vol. 1, p. 845.
26. Ibid.
27. Two fine sources of Sabbath practice for Christians who wish to celebrate it in the context of their own Christian spirituality are Marva Dawn, *Keeping the Sabbath Wholly* (Grand Rapids: Wm. B. Eerdmans Publishing Co., 1989), and Tilden Edwards, *Sabbath Time* (Nashville: Upper Room Books, 1992), both of which are reverent and respectful of the Jewish Sabbath as the original and still central understanding of Sabbath for religious people.
28. Heschel, *The Sabbath,* p. 32.
29. Brueggemann, "The Book of Exodus," p. 846.
30. I have been unable to track down the source of this story.
31. On this point, see H. Boone Porter in *The Day of Light: The Biblical and Liturgical Meaning of Sunday* (Greenwich, Conn.: Seabury Press, 1960), p. 63. Porter notes, "Modern Christendom has not given up any of the specific Sunday actions . . . what it has given up is the principle of *unity* which binds these together. Holy communion has simply become one form of devotion among many, whereas the primitive Eucharist was a comprehensive rite in which the full Gospel was set forth . . . and the fullness of Christian *community* was actually experienced" (italics added).

32. See Jules Isaac, *The Teaching of Contempt: Christian Roots of Anti-Semitism* (New York: Holt, Rinehart & Winston, 1964).

3. Forgiveness as a Way of Being in the World

1. Helen Prejean, *Dead Man Walking: An Eyewitness Account of the Death Penalty in the United States* (New York: Random House, 1993), p. 244.
2. Sharon H. Ringe, *Jesus, Liberation and the Biblical Jubilee* (Philadelphia: Fortress Press, 1985); John Howard Yoder, *The Politics of Jesus* (Grand Rapids: Wm. B. Eerdmans Publishing Co., 1972); André Trocmé, *Jesus and the Nonviolent Revolution* (Scottdale, Pa.: Herald Press, 1973), first published as *Jesus-Christ et la révolution non-violente* (Geneva: Labor and Fides, 1961); Hannah Arendt, *The Human Condition* (Chicago: University of Chicago Press, 1958), esp. pp. 236ff.; Doris Donnelly, *Learning to Forgive* (Nashville: Abingdon Press, 1979, reprint, 1990).
3. See Mortimer Arias, "The Jubilee: A Paradigm for Mission Today," in *International Review of Mission* (Geneva: Commission on World Mission and Evangelism of WCC, January 1984), p. 38.
4. See Ringe, *Jesus, Liberation*, pp. 65–66.
5. Arendt, *The Human Condition,* p. 240. See also Judith Plaskow, *Standing Again at Sinai* (San Francisco: HarperSanFrancisco, 1990), p. 243.
6. See Yoder, *Politics of Jesus*, p. 66. Yoder writes, "Accurately, the word *opheilēma* of the Greek text signifies precisely a monetary debt, in the most material sense of the term. In the 'Our Father' then, Jesus is not simply recommending vaguely that we might pardon those who have bothered us or made us trouble, but tells us purely and simply to erase the debts of those who owe us money; which is to say, practice the Jubilee."
7. Rosemary Radford Ruether, "What World Desperately Needs Is Jubilee Remission of Debts," *National Catholic Reporter* (November 6, 1992).
8. See Joseph Campbell, *The Masks of God* (New York: Viking Press, 1959).
9. Arendt, *The Human Condition,* p. 239.
10. Ibid.
11. Ibid., p. 237.
12. Pope John Paul II, *Reconciliatio et Paenitentiae,* p. 161, quoted in Doris Donnelly, "Some New Thoughts on Penance," in *PACE*

(*Professional Approaches for Christian Educators*) 20 (Huntington, Ind.: Our Sunday Visitor, 1990–91), p. 198. See also Pierre Teilhard de Chardin, *The Divine Milieu* (New York: Harper & Brothers, 1960), p. 24.

13. Elaine Roulet, in private conversation with the author. I do not know the original source of this folktale.

14. Arendt, *The Human Condition,* p. 241.

15. Elie Wiesel, at ceremonies remembering the fiftieth anniversary of the liberation of Auschwitz; "Survivors Pray at Crematories of Auschwitz," *New York Times,* January 27, 1995, sec. A, p. 6.

16. Roger Rosenblatt, *Children of War* (Garden City, N.Y.: Doubleday Anchor Books, 1983), pp. 125–49; esp. p. 148.

17. In an April 27, l995, faculty lecture delivered at Methodist Theological School in Ohio, in Delaware, Ohio, Elaine Ramshaw, professor of pastoral theology, elaborated on this theme, drawing particular attention to inequality of power in situations of sin, such as parents toward children, abusive spouses, and powerful toward powerless persons. Ramshaw draws strong links between forgiveness, violation of boundaries, and the inequality that often characterize those sinning—or abusing—and those sinned against.

18. Ruether, "What World Desperately Needs."

19. See Valerie Saiving, "The Human Situation: A Feminine View," in *Womanspirit Rising,* ed. Carol Christ and Judith Plaskow (New York: Harper & Row, 1979), pp. 29–42. Originally published in *Journal of Religion* (April 1960) © University of Chicago Press, it is Saiving's account of coming to the conclusion that men and women often sinned in different ways because the circumstances of their lives and self-understanding were different.

20. Brian Friel, "The First of My Sins," in Brian Friel, *The Gold in the Sea* (Garden City, N.Y.: Doubleday, 1966), pp. 155–66.

21. See Peggy McIntosh, "White Privilege and Male Privilege: A Personal Account of Coming to See Correspondences through Work in Women's Studies" (paper presented at the Virginia Women's Studies Association conference in April 1986).

22. Lorenz Graham, *How God Fix Jonah* (New York: Reynal & Hitchcock, 1946); recounted by Elaine Ramshaw in "The Best of the Bible Story Books for Children," *PACE* 19 (Winona, Minn.: St. Mary's Press, 1989–90), p. 156.

23. Oscar Romero, *A Shepherd's Diary,* trans. Irene Hodgson (Cincinnati: St. Anthony Messenger Press, 1993), p. 24.

24. Ibid., p. 392.

25. Ibid., p. 522.

26. e.e. cummings, *A Selection of Poems,* with an introduction by Horace Gregory (New York: Harcourt, Brace & World, 1963; reprint, 1965), p. 143.

27. Alice Walker, interview by Charlie Rose, *Charlie Rose,* Public Broadcasting System, November 8, 1993.

28. In June 1995, meeting in general assembly, the Southern Baptist Convention in the United States made a general statement condemning its own history of slavery and its racism and asked for forgiveness from African Americans, past and present.

29. Corrie ten Boom, *The Hiding Place* (Old Tappan, N.J.: Fleming H. Revell Books, 1971), p. 238. I am indebted to Doris Donnelly for this story.

30. Christian Habbe and Donald Koblitz, "Dresden's Undying Embers," *New York Times,* February 12, 1995.

31. As reported in the Gospel of John, these words were spoken by Jesus to Judas at the Last Supper.

32. See Estelle Frankel, "Yom Kippur, Teshuvah, and Psychotherapy," *Tikkun* 9, 5 (Sept.–Oct. 1994): 104.

33. Ibid., pp. 23–24.

34. Prejean, *Dead Man Walking,* pp. 244–45.

4. Proclaim Liberty Throughout the Land to All Its Inhabitants

1. In this section, I am particularly dependent on the work of Sharon H. Ringe; see especially chapter 1 of *Jesus, Liberation, and the Biblical Jubilee* (Philadelphia: Fortress Press, 1985), "Jubilee Traditions in Hebrew Scriptures—A Cluster of Images," pp. 16–32.

2. Ibid., pp. 28ff.

3. See Kathryn Allen Rabuzzi, *The Sacred and the Feminine* (New York: Seabury Press, 1982).

4. Ibid., pp. 100–101; see also pp. 98 and 125.

5. Gilbert Keith Chesterton, *Orthodoxy* (New York: Dodd, Mead & Co., 1908; reprint, 1943), p. 85.

6. The imagery of "seeing through" is James Fowler's; see his *Stages of Faith: The Psychology of Human Development and the Quest for Meaning* (San Francisco: Harper & Row, 1981).

7. Martha Robbins, *Midlife Women and Death of Mother: A Study of Psychohistorical and Spiritual Transformation* (New York: Peter Lang, 1990).

8. Etty Hillesum, *An Interrupted Life: The Diaries of Etty Hillesum 1941–1943* (New York: Pantheon Books, 1983), p. 176.

9. For this citation I am indebted to Australian educator Margaret Woodward of Monash University, Melbourne. I do not know the exact source.

10. Johannes Baptist Metz, *Faith in History and Society* (New York: Seabury Press, 1980), pp. 109–10.

11. (New York: W. W. Norton & Co., 1993).

12. Ibid., p. 29.

13. Ibid., p. 676.

14. Walter C. Kaiser, Jr., "The Book of Leviticus: Introduction, Commentary and Reflections," in *The New Interpreter's Bible* (Nashville: Abingdon Press, 1994), vol. 1, p. 1172.

15. In Marc Gellman, *Does God Have a Big Toe? Stories about Stories in the Bible* (New York: Harper Junior Books, 1989), pp. 1, 3.

16. From chapters 5 and 6 of Julian of Norwich's *Book of Showings,* quoted in Austin Cooper, *Julian of Norwich: Reflections on Selected Texts* (Mystic, Conn.: Twenty-Third Publications, 1988), p. 18.

17. Thomas Berry, in a private conversation with the author.

18. Dom Helder Camera, at a lecture in Melbourne, Australia, April 1985.

19. Elaine Roulet, in a private conversation with the author.

20. Ernest J. Gaines, *A Lesson before Dying* (New York: Random House/Vintage Books, 1993).

21. See Jean Harris, *They Always Call Us Ladies: Stories from Prison* (New York: Charles Scribner's Sons, 1988).

22. See Gretchen Wolff Pritchard, "Good News," *Christian Century* (December 1, 1993): 1203.

23. Ibid.

24. Karen Love, "Cuba's Children," *New York Times,* September 24, 1994, sec. A, p. 23.

25. Anna Quindlen, "Out of the Hands of Babes," *New York Times* November 23, 1994.

26. See Molly Rush, "Living, Mothering, Resisting," *Christianity and Crisis* 40 (December 8, 1980): 348; and Liane Ellison Norman, "Living Up to Molly," *Christianity and Crisis* 40 (December 8, 1980): 341–44.

27. In Rosemary Radford Ruether, *Women-Church: Theology and Practice of Feminist Liturgical Communities* (San Francisco: Harper & Row, 1985), pp. 233–34.

28. For further information, write "Children's Sabbath," Children's

Defense Fund, 122 E Street, Washington, DC 20001; or call
(202) 628–8787.

5. Jubilee Justice

1. The phrase is based on Jesuit Bill Callahan's idea of "noisy contemplation."
2. See Wendell Berry, "Christianity and the Survival of Creation," in *Sex, Economy, Freedom and Community: Eight Essays* (New York: Pantheon Books, 1993), p. 106.
3. See Walter Brueggemann, "Voices of the Night—Against Justice," in Walter Brueggemann, Sharon Parks, and Thomas H. Groome, *To Act Justly, Love Tenderly, Walk Humbly* (New York: Paulist Press, 1986), pp. 5–28.
4. Abraham Joshua Heschel, *The Prophets,* 2 vols. (New York: Harper & Row, 1962); see especially vol. 2, chaps. 1 and 3, especially p. 11.
5. Ibid., vol. 1, p. 3.
6. Ibid.
7. See "Just/Justice," in *Anchor Bible Dictionary* (New York: Doubleday, 1992), vol. 3, pp. 1127–28.
8. John R. Donahue, "Biblical Perspectives on Justice," in *The Faith That Does Justice,* ed. John C. Haughey (New York: Paulist Press, 1977), p. 69.
9. Gerhard von Rad, *Old Testament Theology,* trans. D.M.G. Stalker (New York: Harper & Row, 1962), vol. 1, p. 370; quoted in Donahue, "Biblical Perspectives," p. 68.
10. Donahue, "Biblical Perspectives," p. 69.
11. Ibid.
12. Brueggemann, "Voices of the Night," p. 6.
13. Ibid.
14. See "Jubilee," in *Anchor Bible Commentary* (Garden City, N.Y.: Doubleday, 1981), pp. 1127–28.
15. Ibid.
16. Thomas Berry, *The Dream of the Earth* (San Francisco: Sierra Club Books, 1988), p. 72.
17. Ibid.
18. Wendell Berry, "Christianity," p. 109.
19. Ibid., p. 110.
20. "Camp Lemonade Stand," *New York Times Magazine,* September 4, 1994, p. 15.

21. See Rodolfo Acuna, *Occupied America: The Chicano's Struggle toward Liberation* (San Francisco: Canfield Press/Harper & Row, 1972).

22. See Donella H. Meadows, Dennis L. Meadows, and Jorgen Randers, *Beyond the Limits: Confronting Global Collapse, Envisioning a Sustainable Future* (Mills, Vt.: Chelsea Green Publishing Co., 1992).

23. See Herman Daly, "A Biblical Economic Principle and the Steady-State Economy," *Epiphany Journal* 12 (Winter 1992): 12ff. The comment about the adjunct professors is mine, not Daly's.

24. Editorial, "Palms Down," *New York Times*, October 12, 1994, sec. A, p. 14.

25. Sarah Epperly, in a private communication with the author.

26. Richard Ford, *Wildlife* (New York: Atlantic Monthly Press, 1990), p. 123.

27. Elizabeth Kubler-Ross, *On Death and Dying* (New York: Macmillan, 1969).

28. See Beverly Harrison's inaugural lecture, "The Power of Anger in the Work of Love: Christian Ethics for Women and Other Strangers," *Union Theological Seminary Review* supplement (1981): 41–57.

29. Erich Lindemann, "Symptomatology and Management of Acute Grief," in Robert Fulton, ed., *Death and Identity* (New York: John Wiley & Sons, Inc., 1965), pp. 186–201; reprinted from *American Journal of Psychiatry* 101 (1944): 141–48.

6. Sing a New Song: The Canticle of Jubilation

1. Text printed in the Bulletin of Our Lady of Victory Parish, Bronx, New York, 1995.

2. See *Music from Taizé: Responses, Litanies, Acclamations, Canons*, conceived and edited by Brother Robert; composed by Jacques Berthier (London: Collins Liturgical Publications, 1986), vols. 1 and 2.

3. Words and music for "Jubilee" by Jim Strathdee, in *Jubilee*, 1988 (P.O. Box 1476, Carmichael, CA 95609).

4. Words copyright 1985 by Walter Farquharson; music copyright 1987 by Ron Klusmeier (250 Dundas St. S., Suite 275, Cambridge, Ontario, Canada NIR8A8).

5. Strathdee, *Jubilee*, p. 22.

6. Ibid., p. 12.

7. Ibid., p. 11.
8. See Bob Herbert, "Suffering the Children," *New York Times,* May 27, 1995, p. 19.
9. See Sharon H. Ringe, *Jesus, Liberation and the Biblical Jubilee* (Philadelphia: Fortress Press, 1985).
10. Paula Gunn Allen writes, "We are the land. . . . The land is not really a place separate from ourselves, rather . . . the earth is being, as all creatures are also being; aware, palpable, intelligent, alive" (*The Sacred Hoop: Recovering the Feminine in American Indian Traditions* [Boston: Beacon Press, 1986], pp. 119, 160).
11. Jerry Ryan, "The Pope and the Millennium—I: The News That Didn't Fit, a Repentant Church?" *Commonweal* (October 21, 1994): 6.
12. "Pope Asks Czechs to Forgive Sectarian Wrongs," *New York Times,* May 22, 1995.
13. See Desmond O'Grady, "The Pope and the Millennium—II: The Perils of Penance," *Commonweal* (October 21, 1994): 7.
14. David G. Sansing, ed., *What Was Freedom's Price?* (Jackson, Miss.: University Press of Mississippi, 1978); David W. Blight, *Frederick Douglass' Civil War: Keeping Faith with Jubilee* (Baton Rouge, La.: Louisiana State University Press, 1989); and Stephen B. Oates, *The Fires of Jubilee: Nat Turner's Fierce Rebellion* (New York: Harper & Row, 1975).
15. Margaret Walker, *Jubilee* (New York: Bantam Books, 1966), p. 286.
16. Translations are by Maureen Leach, O.S.F., and Nancy Schreck, O.S.F., *Psalms Anew: A Non-Sexist Edition* (Dubuque, Iowa: The Sisters of St. Francis, 1984).
17. For example, a local parish or congregation, diocese or judicatory, may choose the anniversary of its founding date as the time for proclamation. A family may choose the birth of a new child or grandchild or the death of a patriarch or matriarch. A prayer group may choose the name day or birthday of someone who is a model or mentor to the group. A faculty or a student body may choose a historical event in its school's history that embodies Jubilee traditions. An individual may choose a date with personal meaning such as a christening, a birth, an ordination, or a retirement.
18. See John Howard Yoder, *The Politics of Jesus* (Grand Rapids: Wm. B. Eerdmans Publishing Co., 1972), pp. 34ff.
19. Ibid.
20. "Family Reunion Bridges Gulf of Time and Color," *New York Times,* (May 22, 1995): sec. A, p. 20.

21. Annie Dillard, "An Expedition to the Pole," in *Teaching a Stone to Talk* (New York: Harper & Row, 1982), pp. 40–41. The entire essay is a reflection on liturgical life.

22. If this is a Christian liturgy, with the tradition of Eucharist as its centerpiece, this is the moment for eucharistic Communion; it is, of course, significant that *Eucharist* is translated as "thanksgiving."

23. Louis Dupré, "On Being a Christian Teacher of Humanities," *Christian Century* (April 29, 1992): 455.

24. For an elaboration on this connection, see Gabriel Moran, "Religious Education for Justice," in *Interplay* (Winona, Minn.: St. Mary's Press, 1981), pp. 143–58.

25. One practical way to do this is in groups of sevens: those in the first seven years of life go first; then the eight- to fourteen-year-olds; then those whose oldest are the twenty-one-year-olds; then the twenty-eight's, thirty-five's, forty-two's, forty-nine's, on to those who are past seventy and seventy-seven and eighty-four and ninety-one—counting up their seven years of seven years, as Jubilee tradition requires.

    In addition, the naming need not be individual. Another possibility might be for entire circles to be made up of those who recognize themselves as called to the same vocation. For example, to a leader who asks, "Will those who know the call to prayer respond?" a circle might answer, "We are those people."

Acknowledgments

We are grateful to publishers and copyright holders for permission to use excerpts from the following:

Margaret Walker Alexander, *Jubilee,* copyright ©1966 by Margaret Walker Alexander. Reprinted by permission of Houghton Mifflin Company. All rights reserved.

Jimmy Santiago Baca, *Immigrants in Our Own Land and Selected Early Poems,* copyright ©1982 by Jimmy Santiago Baca. Reprinted by permission of New Directions Publishing Corp.

Sarah Epperly, unpublished material on care for the environment.

Carmelo Erdozain, *La Fiesta del Senor;* ©1979 by Carmelo Erdozain. Published by OCP Publications, 5536 NE Hassalo, Portland, OR 97213. All rights reserved. Used with permission.

Christopher Fry, *A Sleep of Prisoners.* Used with permission of Oxford University Press.

Ron Klusmeier and Walter Farquharson, "Flowers Will Bloom in the Desert."

Jim Strathdee, *Jubilee;* words and music by Jim Strathdee, copyright ©1987 by Desert Flower Music, P.O. Box 1476, Carmichael, CA 95609. Used by permission.

W. B. Yeats, *The Poems of W. B. Yeats: A New Edition,* edited by Richard J. Finneran; copyright ©1934 by Macmillan Publishing Company, renewed 1962 by Bertha Georgie Yeats. Reprinted with permission of Simon & Schuster.

Index of Names and Subjects